Some of Me

(an Anthology)

Papers
Speeches
Poetry and Lyrics
Sermons and Faith

By Elaine Patricia Walker

Printed in the United States of America
ISBN 979-8-9855412-2-9

I dedicate this book to my grandchildren, Micah and Charles-Joseph.

Table of Contents

Forward

In this anthology, the reader will find writings that cover education, religion, politics, mental health, economic issues, myth, leadership, ethics, literacy, rhetoric, learning, art, social justice, grief, philanthropy, various theories, physics, and love.

Being human is a marvelously complicated and thrilling adventure. My interests have taken me to foreign places and have caused me to look deeper, closer to home and self. I am still pondering everything.

The university has been an ideal environment for me. Here, there are so many different ways to examine the world! I advocate for interdisciplinary thinking and collaboration. The alliances across disciplines can produce amazing discovery and opportunities. I want to inspire more exploration and dialogue.

A Soul in Print

by Elaine Patricia Walker

My soul, in its effort to be recognized, lends itself to human language. My identity is expressed in syllables. The symbols that I select to transfer thought, from my mind to the reader, are actually pieces of my soul, pieces of me. My words and I are one.

James E. Miller's essay *Discovering the Self* tells us that language provides the evidence of being. As we communicate with words, the words serve as an extension of the self. It is language that distinguishes the individual. Expression identifies the uniqueness of a person. Simply being, without self-willed expression, does not diminish the value of a human life, but expression certainly animates the human being. I carve out a particular space in the world using tools of communication. This ability I do not take for granted.

Miller believes that the highest stage of development in the process of discovering self can be achieved through the writing process. As we learn to acknowledge and communicate our innermost thoughts, we learn who we are. Miller suggests that a person can arrive at a place of deep self-awareness by examining and recording his/her experiences. Although this exercise is introspective, the result can reach far beyond the individual. The individual matures and becomes a stronger member of their larger community.

Miller argues that language accommodates the human need to express identity and to influence community. Miller's thesis is supported by other authors. Noam Chomsky writes, "...the fundamental human capacity is the capacity and the need for creative self-expression…" (Chomsky, N. 1969. *Linguistics and Politics* - Interview). It is both our ability to express and our need to express ourselves that proves our humanness. The human animal is separated from other animals by this drive to be, and to demonstrate uniqueness through expression. Ernest Cassier also supports Miller's thesis, pointing out the inseparable tie between language and being: "…it is language that makes his [man's] existence in a community possible…" (Cassier, 1946. *Language and Myth*). Community indicates being, settlement, harmony among a group. Language is the central requirement for community. I note that the root of both words; communicate and community, is commune.

The authors I discuss in this paper argue that the state of being involves more than occupying space. To them, "Being" is an active word that requires conscious expression of the self. The authors mentioned here do not include the members of our society/our communities who cannot speak, or write, or participate in common communication processes. I argue that these members of the human family are "being" and that they are as complex and interesting even though they might not express themselves through writing or speech. A person who cannot speak or move their body as they might wish, for example, still experiences thoughts, and the desire to express those thoughts. I hope for a more inclusive description of "being" that acknowledges the different ways humans experience being and communication.

Miller writes that the discovery of language causes the discovery of self. The process of learning to organize thoughts and words, verbally and in writing, helps the individual to see himself/herself clearly. The process of writing and rewriting, thinking and rethinking, causes discovery. I have

found this to be true for me. The more I observe, reflect, read, write, listen, and rewrite - the more I contemplate and think deeply. The more often I think, the closer I come to understanding myself and others.

So, I offer written pieces of myself that can be dissected by the reader who will experience me through my words. Writing is an amazing privilege. Writing serves as a form of self-definition and freedom; from thoughts imprisoned in the mind to thoughts set free through the use of words.

To paraphrase Alfred Whitehead, language is the voice of the soul (*Modes of Thought*, 1938).

If my soul can be observed at all, you will see glimpses of it in the words that I use. My ideas expressed in print preserve my human experience. These same words will stand in my place long after my soul departs the community.

Language is a bridge to one another; spoken, written or observed. We speak without words, soul to soul, gesture to gesture, eye to eye, through dance, and music, and art. Silence is a language as well. All communication is useful for self-discovery.

I agree with Miller that our existence is translated in linguistic terms. The writing process can be a liberating experience that leads to self-discovery and awareness. Our personal journey of discovery will intensify if we dare to write until the words and the soul are one.

-End-

Inequalities in America's Schools

by Elaine Walker, Ed.D.

Nobody told me that I was not as important as Amanda. She had soft, straight, shoulder length blonde hair. She liked science as much as I did. I met her during a school exchange program in the fall of 1966. I did not know that her blue eyes were of greater perceived value than my brown ones. My ignorance about such things shielded me from the color-coded barriers where adults in Amanda's world clashed with the adults in my world. Before Amanda, I was not aware that there were different worlds on the same planet. Clashes between worlds were occurring around the nation as protests regarding school integration raged in America. Amanda and I played hopscotch and sang nursery rhymes as that war raged.

Amanda and I were fast friends during our time together. We loved to learn, to discover. We realized that we looked different, but Amanda and I never thought the differences made one of us more privileged than the other. We did not know that judgments and life-defining decisions were made about us based on our appearance, our address, and where we went to school.

Inequalities exist in America's schools. Much has been written about schools in lower income areas versus schools in higher income areas. The differences are particularly disparate in physical property, supplies and materials for students, resources, equipment, opportunity and faculty. The focus of many writers has been the impact that the inequalities have on the children enrolled in impoverished schools. I was one of those children.

When I was in elementary school, I did not know that I was in a disadvantaged academic environment. By the time that I entered 10th grade, then in high school, I became aware of gross inequality. It was the early 1970s and financial injustice in the school system persisted. I had the chance to visit schools in wealthier zip codes as I competed in a science fair in which I outperformed students from school districts near my home area, and was then allowed to compete further and further away from home. When I returned to my school, which I loved, I noticed how overcrowded classes were. I noticed the brown grass, unkempt grounds, and tattered books. My school library was poorly stocked. We did not have a lot of new things. And no one on my campus looked like Amanda from my elementary school exchange program. I wondered how she was doing. I met so many girls that looked like Amanda, at the sparkling clean, big, bright, well-equipped schools that I visited as a young science scholar.

My lived experiences, in grades K-12, dramatically highlighted the extremes of wealth and poverty as it plays out in America's public school systems. Not much has changed since the time I entered school in 1963. Non-affluent students still struggle with far less than wealthy students who attend well-financed schools. However, students in wealthier school districts are not guaranteed to succeed in their academic, professional, or personal pursuits after high school. Let's reconsider Amanda, my seven-year-old friend from the "better" school.

Amanda attended a private elementary school in an affluent neighborhood. Her father was a surgeon, and her mother was a biologist. Her parents thought it okay for Amanda to be exposed to the less fortunate, for a brief time. That was her time with me, I suppose. After elementary school, Amanda attended an exclusive academy. She wrote letters to me over the years. She had lots of stuff. Her parents owned three homes, one abroad, and lots of cars. She travelled. She received the best education money could buy. Her parents were wealthy (Mom's inherited money and career money earned by her dad). She could buy anything. In her own words, she was lonely, miserable. She told me that she envied me for all I had. How could this be?!

I had very few things. I was raised with both parents and five siblings in a modest home under economically strained circumstances. Before graduating from high school, I had not travelled outside of the state where I was born. The few times my family did travel, it was by car, the only one we owned, to visit with family. The schools I attended were hard pressed for books, equipment, and funds for extracurricular programs. By traditional accounts I was poor, and Amanda was rich. In reality, I was rich, and Amanda was very poor indeed.

Amanda dropped out of college with a 3.8 grade point average. She was a chemistry major with medical school and job connections awaiting her, through her father. She was physically beautiful, smart, well educated, and she came from money. She has been married twice and is recently divorced. She says that she drinks too much. She blames her unhappiness on absentee parents (she was raised by nannies). School has done little to prepare her for a happy life.

My parents and relatives, several of my teachers, neighbors, and friends have provided encouragement and guidance over the years. I saw courageous people go to work every day, demonstrate appreciation for the little we did have, teach values, and share as a community. Wealth was not tied to things and having. To be rich was to be loved. I learned how to respect people based on their ideas and deeds. From a cultural and racial perspective, I was not as isolated as Amanda was because my family embraced diversity and a variety of cultures through marriage. My school mates were racially Black and Latino. Amanda went to school with predominantly White students.

As an adult, I have travelled the world, bought homes, drove my dream car, put a child through college, I ran a business and earned several academic degrees including the Doctorate. I was able, through hard work, to earn money to afford some of the things that Amanda had easy access to her whole life. I am happy, I have a fulfilling career, and I live soberly with purpose. My parents were not able to contribute financially to my education. My parents did not buy me a house, or a car, or anything beyond the clothes I wore as a child, the food I ate in their care, toys I shared with siblings, and the roof over my head they provided until I was of age to go out into the world on my own. My parents loved me in the ways that they could, and they did all that they could to ensure their children made it to adulthood. All of my siblings grew up with good character.

I am saddened by the many children who do fall prey to the pitfalls of poverty, especially those who, in addition to the problems caused by inadequate financial means, also live without love. There are lasting advantages, often underreported, of a loving family unit, of emotional support, and a tight-knit community, in impoverished neighborhoods. Most children reared with love in economically challenged neighborhoods are not bent on self-destruction, or unable to learn, or doomed for failure. They are able to thrive even though their schools are sorely lacking in many areas which means these students have less of almost everything in their school settings, compared to schools in affluent neighborhoods. Imagine what these students could accomplish if they were on equal footing and had equal preparation in school. Financial inequity in America's public schools is alarming. But lack of money is no reason to believe that students can't excel. Money does not make students successful. Amanda, and countless others like her, are proof of that. Money is, however, an important part of the solution to end the unfair financial disparities in America's schools.

As writers highlight what the have-nots do not have, it is equally important to recognize what they do have. There are many brilliant minds with good hearts and great potential, even in the "poorest" school districts. And adults need to tell them so. It does not cost money to tell a child that they are important, valued. No great deal of elaborate preparation or new programs are needed to begin to change our speech. The greatest wealth is realized, not solely in how much we are able to spend, but also in what we say to children in *all* learning environments.

I do not underestimate the benefits of generous finances and access to money for schools. I wish to emphasize that we can instill pride, promote good, and invest in the dignity of all students, wherever they are. I will not wait until our schools have enough money to do this uncomplicated thing: to speak life and hope to our learners. Change, in this case, begins with what we can do now, as we plan and strategize to get the other things our students need.

Amanda, writing from rehab, tells me she is depressed. Both of her parents are still alive and healthy. They are paying for her rehab as she still does not work. Her parents are retired. My father died and my mother is now age 90. I have committed my life to family and the field of Education. The inequities in our school systems drag on.

I still see the same problems in K-12 schools that existed when I first met Amanda in the 1960s. She and I are a case study that continues to stir important questions. Is the public school system in America intentionally designed to give advantages to the wealthier among us? Who really benefits from inequity? How could such unfair practice persist for so long? What will happen to the millions of students in underfunded public schools? What can we do today to cause positive change?

-End-

Never Anywhere

By Elaine Walker (2015)

Humans are experiencing an increasing inability to be fully present. Advances in technology allow us to be incessantly connected and visible to others, but not necessarily extant, not really "there". Consider the example of a parent showing up for their child's ball game, but they ignore the child as they focus on their personal technology. The body can be seen, but the person is not really there. I notice people walking on the street or in buildings and their eyes are focused on their technology. They ignore the people around them. I have sat in meetings where attendees who should give their full attention to the business at hand, are elsewhere, online, engaged with reading, texting, viewing – or otherwise not fully present. I have witnessed people sitting at the same table on a date, or family members sitting together for the purpose of being together, escaping to or lost in virtual worlds, dividing their time in ways that are astoundingly disrespectful to the person in their presence. Sometimes people exchange text messages with a person in the same room instead of using their voices to speak with them. They often make this decision to use texting or electronic messaging when there is no danger or negative consequence if they simply spoke to the person in real time, with their voice.

Technology allows for a perpetual form of presence that simultaneously offers absence. We see people *not being* present. At family dinner tables, or in business meetings, someone disconnects from the reality in front of them and chooses to "be" somewhere else as they respond to or seek some type of active experience with others, by responding to messages, playing games or watching videos, looking at images or joining conversations. It is not the technology that gives me pause, it is the way people use the technology that I find disturbing.

We used to be in one room at one time. We were less prone to distractions. We gave full attention to people in the same room with us who desired to speak with us. We had conversations that had an uninterrupted beginning and end. We thought about our responses before we shared them. We used to be less likely to react hastily to stimuli.

Too many people in my online world share too much, too often. They want to be heard, to unhealthy extremes. Many want to be (now need to be) *seen* by others, strangers included. Modesty is seldom practiced in public online exchanges. The most uninformed opinions are celebrated. Rants and insults are common. Detestable behavior caught on camera becomes popular news, quickly. People are less thoughtful and reflective before they publish an image, claim, or reaction. They respond instantly because they can, not because they should.

Technology is not to blame. We can use technology for good. Misuse of technology by humans is to blame for the decline in social manners, person to person connections, and collaboration that is possible only when we are truly present. Too many people are never anywhere and, to our collective dismay, all over the place, at once. Let's create a new "now" and learn how to arrive, stay, and be there.

Strength to Turn the Page

By Elaine Patricia Walker

This was not the best day for travel, or for cancer, or for war. The President of the United States of America declared war on Iraq three days before Garry went to the hospital complaining of a high fever, unrelated to the war. I needed to get to Garry. The hospital was miles away and I did not have my car. My untimely travels through downtown Los Angeles included pushing past war protestors who were screaming for peace, and squeezing through crowds going in all directions. Everyone was in someone's way. On one of the hottest days, in one of the most polluted sections of town, I pressed and bussed and hiked. There was a peculiar anger in the air. The anger was not confined to the crowds. It met me at the top of the hill at the double glass doors as I entered the hospital.

Garry was admitted to the hospital the day he arrived. Doctors ran blood tests, and they did physical exams. Preliminary results indicated that Garry had some kind of cancer. More tests were needed. Doctors performed a bone biopsy. A week later Garry received a blood transfusion to stabilize his body for the chemotherapy treatments that would begin after the specific cancer was identified. The president of the USA announced that there was a cancer of terrorism spreading and our armed forces would stop it. The doctors said aggressive chemotherapy would attack the cancer cells in Garry's body and kill them before they could do more damage. And so, the wars began.

I gave more attention to the war in Garry's body. I considered the word "chemotherapy." Therapy sounded friendly when in fact it consisted of injections of poison into a suffering body, injections that caused physical and emotional side effects. "Therapy," I sighed. What an inappropriate word for such violence.

From March 30th until the middle of April 2003, Garry endured several types of medical tests, transfusions and mistakes, courtesy of the hospital on the hill. Additional bone marrow biopsy procedures had to be conducted because the samples from the first and subsequent procedures were not good enough to get an adequate reading. Unskilled doctors in training were given opportunities to practice on my brother. Garry endured being awake while a doctor drilled through his bone. These were the details of his war as it began.

On Friday, April 11, 2003, around 4:00 PM, an attending physician informed Garry of the type of cancer that he has. At last, he would learn his enemy's full name. Garry had Mantle Cell Lymphoma. When Garry received the diagnosis a few family members were in his hospital room. Eventually everyone went home. At the end of the day only the cancer stayed in the room with Garry. That night, Garry called me to talk. He felt tired. He wanted to leave the hospital. He wanted the cancer to leave. If only this war was that simple.

Days following the diagnosis, Garry was hooked up to an intravenous apparatus for hydration and nourishment. His body was feverish for weeks. Doctors could not figure out what was keeping his temperature above 100 degrees.

Garry postponed chemotherapy until after he did more research on cancer. Garry was wise to study his enemy. Being prepared made him a soldier instead of a victim.

On Easter Sunday, Garry left the hospital and visited with his family. His frame was frail, but his resolve was strong. It was precious to be with him in my home. War was raging but love provided a reminder of why we oppose invaders, why we fight to protect what we love. We had brief moments of peace on that Sunday.

After his return to the hospital Garry settled in for chemotherapy and seven months of treatments. Therapy consisted of an I.V. drip of three rounds of chemotherapy injected by a needle into the blood stream via an opened vein. Garry reclined in a chair for hours as the neatly packaged poison filled his body in three 8-hour sessions, over a three-day period, Wednesday through Friday. After the three days of treatments, Garry recuperated and prepared for the next round of treatments scheduled each month until September.

The hospital discharged Garry after his first series of treatments. He would return to the hospital every Tuesday for a check-up. After 28 days he would start another three-day series of chemotherapy until he reached the 7th month mark. Garry survived the first series of treatments. Nausea and chills were eased with medication. With rest, his stamina increased. His humor resurfaced. He fought his enemy as I secretly cried and trembled.

Years earlier, I had already lost my twin brother, Garry's only older brother, to a dreadful disease. Five years later our father died. I prayed so diligently for the life and health of my twin who died a horrible death anyway. I prayed for more years with my father, but he died just the same. I was so deeply afraid that I would lose Garry. I felt guilty for thinking about how I felt, when Garry was fighting for his life. It was not about me, or my precious mother, who might have to bury yet another son, or my siblings who would have to say goodbye to another brother, or our family and friends whose lives would change forever without Garry. It was about Garry, and him getting better, and him being cancer free. And I shouldn't worry that the cancer could return even if he gets to remission. And I shouldn't be gripped with fear because fear meant that I lacked faith, that I was giving up and Garry was still here. So I snapped out of it for hours at a time and reached out for my brother.

As the month of May began, Garry and I attended movies, we went to restaurants, and we visited bookstores together. Garry's appetite was good. He told jokes again. Garry is one of the funniest people in the world. I allowed his stories and recollections of our childhood to cover us. We needed the humor. Laughing was our normal. Normal was necessary during this wicked season of war. Our normal helped me to accommodate his cancer. It was our cancer now.

There were all kinds of wars raging, all dangerous but not necessarily in the news. I tried to cope with the variety of wars in my life. No one knew my struggle with physical pain. I suffered quietly because I did not want to avert attention from Garry's war. How could I fight all of the wars at once? How could I understand why they were necessary or better than peace?

The first weeks of June were grey. Low clouds covered everything and blocked the sun. It was fitting that nature acknowledge Garry's cancer and adjust accordingly. July brought the heat. Garry was out of the hospital, and he was getting out of the house often. On July 12th Garry attended my graduation ceremony. The next day he and I went to a movie and enjoyed the day together. This war had not crushed our history, nor ruined our bond. We dared to talk about the future.

On Monday, July 14th, Garry was scheduled for another bone biopsy and a heart test. His formally enlarged spleen was shrinking, and blood test results looked promising. It was time to see if the cancer cells were dying and staying dead. We celebrated cautiously as he entered another round of procedures.

On Wednesday, July 30th, having finished his third chemo treatment the week before, Garry began vomiting at 4:00 A.M. and continued all day long. He was taken to the hospital, examined, hydrated, and given drugs intravenously. He was exhausted, sore, bewildered. No one could pinpoint why his body so violently betrayed him. If it were the chemo drugs, they would have caused such a reaction shortly after the initial treatment. It was not likely due to something he had eaten. Garry is a vegetarian, a runner, and other than the cancer, a very healthy man.

After three days Garry was back to his better self. Soon his birthday rolled around. August 9th took on great significance. Surviving another year demanded celebration. Instead of a big party with lots of people, Garry and I spent time together alone. We met for a movie then chatted over dinner. This was fine with me. I wanted to give him undivided attention. I did not know how to tell him how much I loved him. How much he mattered.

At Garry's leading, we did not talk about the cancer. Talking about it might have made it bigger. He needed that enemy to appear weak and conquered. We talked about the other war. The dictator's sons killed in a shoot-out. The dictator caught hiding in a hole in the ground. We discussed the politics and insanities of that kind of war and the rationale for defense. We talked about other things, anything, other than the cancer.

From mid-August to early October, Garry completed his chemotherapy. The cancer treatments were effective. We celebrated as if we had finally won this war. The first week in October, Garry endured yet another bone biopsy and series of tests. Garry called me at 7:00 P.M. on Tuesday, October 7th to report that the mantle cells were now replaced by healthy cells. His spleen was normal size again. The final week of October, Garry would have only one more round of treatments. On November 14th he would complete his final series of tests. It looked good.

On Saturday evening, October 18th, Garry told me that a stem cell process and the most extreme doses of chemotherapy would follow the seven months of treatment he had already endured. The doctor informed Garry that this more aggressive therapy was necessary to prevent relapse. Garry was shocked by this news because he was led to believe that the cancer was fully arrested over the past seven months. Although he would be tracked for five years, he was confident that the cancer would not resurface. Now Garry was told that a cancer patient who presented with the same symptoms Garry had, experienced a relapse after less than two years. The doctors wanted to be proactive. Dreadful news. I did not want to carry it as we walked at the event we would attend on Sunday.

Garry and I and other family members and friends would participate in a fundraiser walk for AIDS research. We had lost our brother to AIDS and the world had lost too many to this disease. The good news was that Garry would be healthy enough to walk. The bad news was that his cancer would be there too. Garry did the walk and kept us laughing throughout that day.

Over time, Garry became stronger. He had physical therapy for bone damage in one of his shoulders, additional medication and a few more treatments. Finally, the cancer was in remission and there were no new surprises.

I could take no credit for Garry's progress. I did not stand against the illness, undaunted. I did not pray with confidence. The cancer might come back. I was weakened by the past. From 2003 to 2011 the war in Iraq and the Middle East continued. Thousands of civilians and soldiers died in that war, and because of the battles and attacks that emanated from it. Garry lived.

Garry's war paralyzed me. I could not seem to move past my fear of losing him. I knew that life would go on, as it has since my other brother's death, and my father's death, and the many other deaths of relatives and friends. I know that death is a natural part of the human experience. I can understand it, intellectually. Somehow, the deaths of my twin brother and father changed me. Garry's death, I was afraid, would undo me. It is a very selfish supposition. I did not want to be selfish, ever. Garry's cancer was about Garry and his importance and his perspective, and his healing. I realize more perfectly that Garry is so much a part of me. If that part of me left this world, I dreaded the emptiness that would remain. I tried to focus on the fact that Garry is still here. He is changed also, but still here. We can get back to doing what we love.

Garry and I both love to read. During Garry's first battle with cancer, I found it very difficult to read the book I love the most; the Bible. The bible is filled with amazing history, wisdom, and promises. The bible usually comforts me. So often, when I attempted to read passages during Garry's illness, my eye would always be drawn to stories of wars and battles in the bible. I hate violence, so those accounts made me sad. I was already sad. I pondered war and its place in this life. I wished that war was never practiced. I wished it was not necessary.

But war was necessary, and it was personal. I had to declare war against a merciless enemy that tried to kill my brother. The enemy's name is cancer, and it is not merely a group of out-of-control cells doing damage. This enemy has ravaged and killed thousands. This enemy attacked someone I love. Like a group of terrorists bent on destruction, cancer too had to be stopped.

I began to pray with renewed determination for my brother and my country. I found the strength to lift my bible, open it, read the first book and chapter about beginnings, and that gave me the strength to turn the page. The stories of wars were still there, but I was drawn more to the accounts of deliverance, healing, miracles, victory, peace, and hope. This was a beginning, again, for Garry. Remission meant time to recover, time to reflect. Time to get past mere survival, to live.

After a period of remission, Garry was pronounced "cured." How could we be sure that the cells would not run wild again? Did we get them all? Were new ones starting up? I had faith but I also had experience. I cautiously returned to the routine of my living. The routine included dealing with other wars, including the so-called "War on Terror." From years 2001-2016 the United States of America has led counter-terrorism activity, prompted by the September 11, 2001 attacks on American soil. In December 2014, NATO (North Atlantic Treaty Organization) formally ended combat operations in Afghanistan, marking the beginning of a new phase of the conflict. The withdrawal of US troops from Afghanistan, as well as NATO troops, and the gradual transfer of combat roles from NATO forces to

Afghan security forces, occurred between 2011 and 2014. President Barak Obama announced that U.S. combat operations in Afghanistan would end in December 2014, with a plan to remove all residual U.S. forces by the end of 2016. Former President George Bush was in office when the "War on Terror" began. President Obama was in his last term of office (2016). We were still at war.

As a nation, we join other assaulted and concerned countries as we continue to fight the cancer of terrorism. America is worried about growth of uncontrolled radical cells. Me too. Coincidentally, Garry again found himself at war with his body. October 2015 is when Garry admitted that the cancer had returned. However, Garry would not work with doctors that practiced traditional cancer therapies. He had already tried chemotherapy and radiation, bone biopsies and transfusions. He did not ever plan to repeat those types of treatments. Those who knew Garry best honored his decision. Close family and friends tried to offer alternatives and assistance. From late 2015 to late 2016, Garry's body gave clear signs that it was in decline. Cancer cells multiplied. Doing nothing equally aggressive to fight the cancer allowed for unchecked invasion. I felt terror as I watched Garry's health decline. I could not figure out how to ignore the cancer.

The cancer grew brazen as it survived chemo and four US Presidents. Our family surrounded the cancer and loved Garry through every battle, through every bad day. Garry and I talked about everything important to him, as cancer sat in the room with us. We discussed the 2016 election for President of the United States of America. We watched the 2017 swearing in of the controversial president. Garry loved to talk politics.

The day before Valentine's Day 2017, Garry and I spoke for 2 hours about his pending projects (film work, scripts), the awards season (Golden Globes, Oscars, Grammy's). We talked about the great friends he had, topics in history, our past, and his future. We promised to visit the day after Valentine's Day. We did get together. What an unforgettable meeting!

On February 15, 2017, I stood at Garry's bedside in the emergency room. Prior to his arrival at the hospital, he was alone at home and had called 911 for help. An ambulance rushed him to the hospital after stomach pain persisted. Doctors determined that his spleen had ruptured. He was bleeding internally. Only surgery could repair that. Garry's body was not stable enough for surgery. Cancer had ravaged him. His body shut down. I was there for several of Garry's cardiac arrests and related procedures to resuscitate. Eventually family gathered and we all said our goodbyes.

What cancer did to my brother and to our family and his friends was a most memorable terror. Garry's funeral was held on Friday, March 3, 2017. He was 55 years old. Garry had a great life. We celebrate this brilliant man, as we endure the terrorist that is cancer.

-END-

Papers

Adult Literacy in the United States of America

1990s to 2020s
A 30-Year Retrospective

Editor: Elaine Patricia Walker, Ed.D.

Executive Summary

From the 1990s to the 2020s adult literacy has increased for adults living in the United States of America. Adult literacy assessments and reporting have also increased. The definition of Literacy has expanded to include fluency with online communication.

There are readily available computer-based programs (software) that can translate spoken words and images into written text. The learning of reading and writing and word recognition are simplified by user-friendly methodologies. Technology has enabled more people to have access to reading instruction and practice. Public libraries and grant-funded programs allow free access to technology. With these advancements, adult literacy rates are improving.

Over the past 30 years, educators and researchers of adult literacy have documented competency levels in written and spoken communication. What we write and how we speak has taken on increased importance in the 21st century. From political messaging to personal expression, words are at the center of discourse that impacts our safety, our opportunities, and the public good.

This adult literacy study offers samples from the research, for discussion and analysis. Featured in Section I is The Library Adult Reading Program, popular in the 1990s.

Section I: The 1990s

by
Elaine Walker, Ed.D.

Adult Literacy
in the
United States of America

A 30 Year Retrospective

Elaine Patricia Walker, Ed.D.

Adult Literacy
The Library Adult Reading Project:
An Approach to Teaching the Adult New Reader

TABLE OF CONTENTS

Introduction of Adult Illiteracy in Contemporary America

Review of the Literature

Research shows that literacy is inextricably tied to professional and social success, as defined in contemporary American culture (Jackson, R. & Harris, J. 1983). The ability or inability to read, often determines the type of work a person can do, the salary they can earn, and the ease with which they move through everyday life. The Ohio Literacy Resource Center reports that 41% to 44% of adults in America who are in poverty, according to federal poverty guidelines, are also illiterate (1998). The National Institute of Education (Washington, D.C.) and the National Adult Literacy Survey (Princeton, NJ) report that 50% of the chronically unemployed are not functionally literate. "It is estimated that limited literacy skills cost businesses and taxpayers $20 billion in lost wages, profits, and productivity, annually" (Kirsch, I. & Jungelblut, A. 1996).

How well do adults need to read, to survive in modern society? Following are a few examples of required reading levels that researchers have confirmed. Reading skills at the 6th grade level are required to read and understand a driver's license manual. To read and understand most frozen TV dinner instructions requires a 4th grade reading level. Microwave

31

heating instructions of food containers have been simplified by the addition of pictures, but reading is still required. Directions on an aspirin bottle are written at the 6th grade level. To read and understand most apartment rental contracts requires 12th grade reading skills. A 7th grade reading level is required to understand public/online newspaper content. Almost all jobs in the minimum wage category require reading skills. A supply/stock clerk requires 5th grade level reading skills. A maid (who uses cleaning agents) needs 6th grade reading skills to work safely. According to researcher Paul Pearson, author of *The Future of Work and Education,* reading and work are related. A literate adult population can save America billions of dollars in remedial retraining of its work force.

Reading ability affects state and national economics.

Reading ability is also tied to self-esteem. Studies have shown a link between ability to read and self-perception and social behavior. The U.S. Department of Education and the National Assessment for Education Progress reports that 60% of America's adult prison inmates are functionally illiterate, and 85% of all younger offenders ages 15-19 have problems reading. Most illiterate adults were once illiterate children. Most illiterate children who are enrolled in public schools in America suffer from low self-esteem which can cause behavioral difficulties, such as disruptive behavior in the classroom, masking of frustration through bullying, and chronic truancy.

The literature has demonstrated a clear connection between literacy and progress in contemporary American society. Reading skills enable citizens to function within American society, which uses written words in almost every context of shared public life. From instructions on medicine bottles, to traffic signs, to online, words are everywhere. An adult who cannot read is severely disadvantaged. Literacy is strongly associated with economic success. An individual's literacy level can indicate their success in the labor market. Researchers agree that adult literacy also has an impact on national progress.

National and State Statistics

The US. Department of Education reports that 1 in 5 (20%) of American adults is functionally illiterate. In addition to the 20% functional illiteracy rate, another 34% of American adults are only marginally literate. A 1991 publication of The English Language Proficiency Study presented by Laubach Literacy Action Council, indicated that approximately 13% of American adults (as many as 21 million people), age 20 and over, do not read at all, or they read below the 4th grade level. Johnathan Kozol, researcher, and author of *Illiterate America* says 75% of unemployed adults have reading difficulties. He also says that 50% of American adults are unable to read an 8th grade level book.

A 1989 study of 3,600 adults ages 21 to 25, conducted by The National Assessment for Education Progress, indicated the following: 80% could not read a bus schedule, 73% could not accurately interpret a newspaper story, 63% could not follow written map directions, 28% could not write a billing error letter, and 23% were unable to locate the gross pay-to-date on a paycheck stub.

Approximately 2.2 million people (44,000 per week) are added to the adult illiterate population of America, every year. The United Nations indicates that the United States ranks 49th among 156 United Nation member countries in its rate of literacy (a drop of 18 places since 1950).

The statistics on adult literacy have meaningful implications for America's future.

Implications

Traditional job and career patterns are dissolving as the knowledge content of jobs evolves and the need for low-skill workers fades. As business and labor markets change, some jobs become obsolete and new ones are created. A demand for more literate workers is a requirement of the new, global community. People will be required to have multiple skills if they will excel in the global job market (The Organization for Economic Cooperation and Development. 1998). Literacy, in this context, is key.

Research confirms that literacy has an effect on the ability of workers to learn efficiently and to be flexible in learning. It also has an effect on the rate at which a culture of lifelong learning can be realized. According to the OECD, a country's ability to compete in the new, global economic environment, depends on the knowledge and skills of the population. "People are the key resource, and their level of literacy is a powerful determinant of a country's innovative and adaptive capacity. Cultivating and developing literacy should be an important element in every country's long-term policy strategies" (1998).

The literature and the statistics bear out the need for programs to help nonreading adults. The next section highlights some of the challenges of attempting to reach and serve this population.

The Challenges of Addressing the Problem of Adult Illiteracy

<u>Reaching the Adult New Reader</u>

One of the key findings of the International Adult Literacy Survey (Canada, 1995), was that adult education and literacy training programs are less likely to reach individuals with low literacy skills, as most training goes to those with high skills. Adult new readers, who need instruction and special assistance in literacy training, are least likely to seek help (Library Adult Reading Project. 1999). Many adults who are functionally literate, do not seek help to improve their reading skills. They "get by".

Some adults exhibit signs in their behavior that might indicate illiteracy, or a serious deficiency as a reader. These behaviors are often masked:

1. They ask people (even people they don't know) to fill out forms for them
2. They make lots of mistakes when they fill out forms for themselves
3. They take forms home instead of filling them out in public

4. They make excuses for not reading in public ("I forgot my glasses...")
5. They repeatedly ask someone to explain what they just read
6. Their eyes fail to move from left to right while reading
7. They fail to respond to written notices, bills, etc.
8. They continually "forget" appointments, even when they have written reminders
9. They do not write letters, or use technology to print out messages in full
10. They turn down opportunities that might require reading or writing

The challenge is getting adults who do not read well to seek help. There is a stigma associated with illiteracy. Adults who cannot read are considered second class citizens. Feelings of embarrassment and inadequacy plague many adults who struggle with reading. Who are these adults who can't read? According to the national Adult Literacy Council, English-speaking whites in America make up the top 41% of adult nonreaders. English-speaking blacks comprise 22%, and native Spanish-speakers also 22%. Only 15% are other non-English speakers. Forty-four percent of America's illiterate adults were over age 50 (in 1996) and ages 45 and older in 2020.

There are programs designed to assist illiterate and partially literate adults. Some of the programs require new readers to attend sessions at public libraries, or to come to other locations where anonymity is not guaranteed. Some of the literacy programs must close down because of limited or discontinued funding. In 1986-87, the federal government spent $17.00 per illiterate adult to aid adult literacy efforts. Tax dollars and private grants fund literacy programs, but the illiteracy rates among the adult population in America, continues to grow. For those adults who will seek help, regardless of the hurdles, there are reading programs available.

The Library Adult Reading Project is a Los Angeles based program which is designed to assist adults who desire to improve their reading skills. This program directly addresses the research topic of adult literacy. The program's mission is to serve as a solution to adult illiteracy. This research study examines the teaching methods, the curriculum, and the materials that the program utilizes as well as the programs' criteria for assessment.

The Library Adult Reading Project

Overview

The Library Adult Reading Project is a non-Profit program operated by the Los Angeles Public Library. There are twenty-one libraries in Los Angeles County that offer LARP reading programs, with fully equipped reading centers for adults. Each reading center is staffed by a LARP coordinator and volunteers trained to provide private instruction. LARP trains volunteers to tutor adults in reading and writing skills. Materials, as well as training for tutors and students, are free. Any adult, age 16 or older, who can speak and understand English, and needs assistance with basic literacy skills, is eligible as a student in the program.

Tutors work as volunteers. Tutors must attend an orientation meeting, an interview, and a 12-hour training workshop in Laubach Literacy methods. Volunteers tutor a minimum of twice each week. They must make a six-month commitment to the program. Refresher and extended training is also available to volunteer tutors.

LARP estimates that 750,000 people in Los Angeles cannot read or write English well enough to meet their daily needs. They experience difficulty when filling out forms, reading street signs, writing letters, paying bills, or helping their children with homework. Adult illiteracy is recognized as a problem that directly or indirectly affects all society. The LARP program places great emphasis on the importance of reading and writing skills, as these skills relate to the quality of life for all citizens. The LARP program desires to be part of the solution to the problem of adult illiteracy.

LARP's Basic Philosophy for Tutors

LARP insists that tutors have "genuine devotion to, and concern for students". Tutors should attempt to "build a ladder of successful learning experiences. This gives students a more positive self-image, based on greater self-confidence and improved competence." (Laubach, F., Tutor's Manual. 1989)

According to LARP, rapport and success are the keys to relating well with students. The program teaches tutors that no learning, of any kind, can take place until the tutor creates a relaxed, friendly atmosphere with the student. Further, the student's feelings of success are one of the most important aspects of the tutoring process. "Success raises one's level of aspiration". It is the tutor's responsibility to create an environment in which "success" can be realized by the student. Tutors are to look for the gains in skills, however small, that are the evidence of growth and encourage their student in them. Each session is expected to be a rewarding experience for both student and tutor. The student should experience some definite success in each lesson. Tutors are expected to give praise for student achievement, but they are also cautioned to be honest so that the praise will be meaningful. To this end, tutors are expected to present lessons in ways in which the student can succeed. This philosophy places lots of responsibility on the tutor. I will discuss the implications of this in the section on critique of the LARP program.

The foundation for the program is loyalty to adult literacy, and high commitment to students. Tutors must submit a monthly report of progress. Accountability is very important. The program is founded on the teaching philosophy of Dr. Frank Laubach.

Teaching Strategies of the LARP Program

Sight Words are practiced to reduce as much as possible the burden of unknown words that confronts the student. The 300 most frequently used words in the English language make up 65% of all written materials. It is suggested that tutors help students to make flash cards of these words using manuscript writing (printing). Tutors introduce no more than ten words at a time. Tutors help students to divide the words into three stacks: known, unknown, and doubtful. Words from the "doubtful" stack are practiced first, as known words are mixed in. Again, an emphasis on student success is underscored. In this light, tutors spend no more than 10 minutes per session on new words. Long periods of drilling are not recommended, as students may become overwhelmed. Tutors also introduce social sight words, such as "Exit Only", "One Way", "In Case of Emergency", "Wet Paint", "Push to Open", "Out of Order", and so forth. A tutor's main focus is helping students to read words that are important to survival in every day urban and "online" life.

Reinforcement and review is used to help students experience progress. Tutors are instructed to reinforce a particular skill with which the student has difficulty. Tutors review material as often as is necessary, but also advance in the lesson to ensure that students move through at least one Skill Book within a six-month period. There are six Skill Books ranging from beginning to intermediate. The books have reading lessons and exercises in them. Students use these books at each session, along with other materials such as newspapers, bills, or any other item of personal importance to the student. Tutors utilize students' materials, to make reading more meaningful for the students.

Writing, to reinforce reading, is particularly stressed in the program. Writing reinforces mastery of newly learned words. This practice enables the student to transfer skills learned from the workbook to other settings. Students write letters, answer ads, create resumes, and work on other similar practical applications. Those students with beginning skills are asked to write words or phrases associated with pictures they are shown. Students write from their own experiences. Tutors encourage students to write in any style that interests them (poetry, stories, a journal).

The "language experience" approach is also utilized. In this activity the student dictates a sentence or tells a story which the tutor prints exactly as dictated. They review what was written. The goal here is vocabulary development.

The student is guided in role playing ("If I were a doctor, I would…"), to experiment with and learn new words. Tutors also ask students to copy unknown words that they see around their homes, or in public places. These words become part of the lesson.

Speech sounds, speech patterns, and phonic-based instruction is part of the teaching strategy. Students start the program with Skill Book 1, which utilizes phonics. Students must be able to pronounce short and long vowel sounds, consonant sounds, and recognize sight words, before moving on to the next skill level.

Tutors also use Word Patterns (words with rhyming end patterns, such as h<u>and</u>) to help students stretch their vocabulary. Word Pattern exercises are introduced in Skill Book 1 and reinforced through Skill Books 2 and 3.

"Duet" reading is another teaching strategy of the LARP program. This strategy is designed for students who have some reading ability but who are reading hesitantly, word for word, or with no expression. The tutor helps the student to select an item of interest to the student (homework from his/her child, an invoice, a letter from work). The tutor reads aloud with the student, using expression in his/her voice. The tutor follows punctuation closely, and reads at a normal rate, even if the student hesitates. The idea is that after a few sessions, it will become easier for the student to keep up.

Tutors are strongly advised to listen to the student. Lessons should be centered around the student's needs (i.e., job, family life, health, legal rights or concerns, etc.). All goals should aim at meeting the student's more immediate needs. Tutors are also asked to be prepared with a list of local referrals for dealing with special problems such as:

• Psychiatric help	• Housing	• Immigration issues
• Economic assistance	• Special health problems	• Legal matters
• Employment	• Family Counseling	• Food Programs
• Insurance	• Taxes	• Childcare

LARP utilizes the Laubach Literacy program as the basis for all adult literacy training and instruction. This teaching strategy has been used since 1969 and has been expanded over the years. A complete set of guidelines and explanations are provided for all tutors during training. Tutors are expected to refer to the instructional materials throughout their service as volunteer literacy tutors.

Assessment of the LARP Program

Criteria for Assessment

The LARP Program uses informal testing to measure student achievement. The rate at which students experience progress in learning, is monitored by the tutor and reviewed periodically by a coordinator. The student's advancement through the skills workbooks is marked by regular review sessions with the tutor. Results are reported and compiled. Students receive a certificate which acknowledges their completion of each skill workbook. The criterion for assessment is determined by the LARP program.

The Significance of Who Defines and Measures the Success of the Program

LARP allows each student to define "success" for themselves. Students come to the program with different goals, and different levels of reading and writing ability. One student might want to improve writing skills, while another might not read or write at all. This approach allows for great latitude in measuring "success".

The program uses the Laubach Way to Reading, which emphasizes compassion over strict standards. There is no outside agency that determines the success of the program. Success is not based on standardized measurement. Students are not compared to other students at similar ability levels.

Assessment consists of program generated "benchmarks" or goals which guide the instruction. If a student learns at least five new words per week, for example, and accomplishes a personal goal, this student is considered to be "successful".

It is significant that LARP does not use outside agencies to measure their success as literacy tutors. Objective investigation and standard measurements might lend credibility to their reports of "success" in reducing illiteracy in the adult population.

Critique of the LARP Program

There is no way to determine the long-range effect of the LARP program on sustained reading progress. Formal testing is not used. Students are not required to be tested over time. The program does not track student progress for longer than one year following the student's completion of the last skill book.

The tutor training assumes that tutors themselves are able to teach. The tutors work very closely with students, often becoming aware of emotional or personal problems the students have. The program assumes that tutors are themselves emotionally and socially mature, and that tutors know when to refer. LARP Tutors are often called upon to serve as counselors during literacy sessions. LARP needs better pre-screening of tutor applicants.

<u>Praise for the LARP Program</u>

LARP encourages a learning environment free from the stress of test-taking, timed progress, or routinized lesson plans that do not fit every student. The student helps to determine what the goals are, and the lessons can be customized. Adult new readers are frequently able to realize progress almost immediately. Instruction is free. There is no time limit for the program so learners do not feel rushed. Learners may receive one-on-one instruction, which can help to engage the student.

Summary of Findings/Conclusion

The National Center on Adult Literacy continues to conduct research that investigates reading and writing ability among the adult population in America. According to their findings, the state of California ranks high in adult illiteracy. The LARP seeks to address this problem by offering tutoring in basic reading and writing skills. The program has trained more than 10,000 tutors throughout the county of Los Angeles. The program can not specifically report the progress of its students who entered the program because not all students complete all levels of instruction in a set period of time. Students may pause indefinitely, taking breaks from tutoring sessions, and still be considered "students" of the program.

Future Research and Challenges

An objective assessment of the program will require an outside agency. Self-reporting is not as credible. Professional counselors, serving as active advisers, might relieve tutors from duties they are not trained to handle. The absence of training or adequate supervision from professional counselors could put the program at risk for legal suits. A formal follow up program might prove useful for assessment measures. LARP is funded, in part, from government grants. It appears to be a viable program that might benefit from more careful preparation of its tutors, and a better follow-up program to track student outcomes.

Bibliography

Barton, P.E. (1998). *ETS policy notes.* ETS Policy Information Center. Princeton, NJ. pic@ets.org http://www.ets.org

Coley, R. (1996). OECD Publications & Information Center. Washington, D.C.

Davis, A. & McDaniel, T. *Teaching reading: an essential vocabulary.* The Reading Teacher. Vol. 52, No. 3. Nov. 1998.

Institute for Educational Leadership. (1980). *Statistics on adult literacy.* IEL@netscape.

Jackson, R. & Harris, J. (1983). *A consideration of social and economic costs to citizens.* South Carolina Literacy Association.

Kaplan, D. (1996). *Adult literacy studies.* National Center on Adult Literacy. http://www.udel.edu/ETL/SARA/tech.rept.html

Kirsch, I. & Jungleblut, A. (1986). *Literacy Profiles of America's Young Adults.* Princeton. Educational Testing Service.

Laubach Literacy Action Council. (1998). U.S. Program of Laubach Literacy International. Syracuse, NY.

Library Adult Reading Project (LARP). (1999). Los Angeles Public Library.

Miller, D. (1996). *Learner-centered community based adult literacy education.* A Comparison of Reading Methodologies. University Press. NY.

National Adult Literacy Survey. (1992).

Organization for Literacy, Economy, and Society. (1995). International Adult Literacy Survey.

Pearson, P. (1997). *The future of work and education.* Cambridge Press. IL.

Pendleton, A. (1998). *Young adult literacy and schooling: A summary report.* National Center for Education Statistics.

Section II: The 2000s

Adult Literacy in the
United States of America

A 30-Year Retrospective

The 2000s

<u>Introduction</u>

The Institute of Education Sciences (IES) and the National Center for Education Statistics publishes annual reports that provide research findings that inform activity and progress in the field of Education.

This 30-year retrospective includes results from Assessment efforts: featuring <u>Basic Reading Skills and the Literacy of America's Least Literate Adults.</u> (2003. NAAL).

Data from The National Assessment of Adult Literacy and the American Institutes for Research provide insights that help to explain progress, deficiencies, and areas for concern as we contemplate adult illiteracy in the United States of America.

Researcher Elaine Patricia Walker continues to promote collaborative work with the U.S. Department of Education, and Adult Literacy Programs for a strong workforce.

An Analysis of David Hume's *Of the Standard of Taste*

The Concept of "Better" in Art Observation
By: Elaine Walker

Hume argues "…judgements of taste are emotional in nature and necessarily subjective, but that some judges are better than others." (Ward, Lock. 1898). What are the implications of "better" in a society where everyone's sentiments are right, but everyone's opinions are not equal? Hume offers several arguments in his essay, Of the Standard of Taste. I have included an overview of those arguments which I interpret as most relevant to this discussion. In this article, I focus on the concept of "better" in art observation.

Hume asserts that comparison is necessary in the development of good taste, or for that matter, "better" taste. Comparison in this context is a scientific exercise of applying a suitable standard that is so determined by a majority of experts. Hume would argue that observation, practice, and comparison are tools of the best critics. To clarify Hume's argument, it is helpful to compare it to Plato's writing on the same subject. Hume disagrees with Plato.

Hume's departure from Platonic thought is important. Hume, a philosopher committed to empiricism, challenged Plato's argument concerning intellectual truth in perception. Metaphysical speculation was

53

diminished by Hume's approach. Plato might disagree with Hume's claim that all moral judgments are based in sentiment; that they are not intellectual judgements. Where Hume says that work can be beautiful, Plato says that this is not possible because beauty is not *in* the object. Plato regards beauty as an ideal. "Beauty exists only in the mind" says Hume, and "each mind perceives a different beauty." For Hume, there is no absolute, ideal beauty, only consensus that the observable is "good". If we propose that Hume makes the stronger argument regarding beauty and judgement, it is interesting then to note his comments concerning "good taste" and his suggestion that men should establish a consensus on the matter of the beautiful or "the better". Before consensus can be reached (consensus as the act of agreement about a standard), it would help if everyone agreed on a basic technique for observing art. Plato says one must try to escape the object, to go beyond it. Do not take the object or artifact on its own terms. Hume says, "To enable a critic the more fully to execute this undertaking, he must preserve his mind free from all prejudice, and allow nothing to enter into his consideration but the very object which is submitted to his examination." We begin our dialogue in intellectual disagreement, thus the excitement of Hume!

As I read Hume's essay again and again, the concept of "better" emerges. Hume wrote, "…every individual ought to acquiesce in his own sentiment, without pretending to regulate those of others." For Hume, we regulate taste but not sentiment. Taste, good taste, equals good judgment, which can be developed or learned. As Ward and Lock observe [Hume's] "essay... (1757) confronts the question of whether taste can be legitimated through rational argument". Hume's explanation of sentiment centers on individualism. Sentiment is of the mind, the whim. It is not fixed. Sentiment is too personal a thing to regulate. Taste, which involves physical qualities, is for Hume, measurable. Good taste, then, is attainable.

Hume offers critical appraisal of what we don't know with our senses, and what we do know with our intellect. Hume says that our sense of reality is a sort of construct where habitual observations merge with what we feel. From this, standards are constructed. The highest standards of taste are set by those who consciously practice observation.

Hume intellectualizes "good" taste. His argument is rational to the extent that he clarifies his use of the word "better" as it refers to the critic. The ability to discern very minute, small, delicate features in things is that which raises the level of "superiority". The discerning critic, the better critic, is the one who has developed an ability to recognize nuances. This ability comes from the disciplined practice of careful observation. In essence, one can *become* better. Plato, with his belief in hierarchy, might agree in part with Hume on that point. Plato would caution that all men are not able to reach the higher levels of understanding (of discernment). The philosopher learns to apprise the beautiful ideal form and learning is a process of "becoming better".

The concept of "better" is detected in Hume's assertion that comparison and consensus comprise the standards of good taste. The idea of consensus is of great interest to me as I examine Hume's essay. How do we account for fairness in judgment, in the body of the unique, or among those with minority opinions?

Is "better" more correct? Does better require majority consensus to confirm its "rightness"? Does better exist apart from human intervention? Is better moved by human words and whim? Does better change? Can better be manipulated by the most persuasive rhetoric? Consensus begins with one man whose conclusions seem right to another. When two or more agree, is this when better joins them? There is something troubling about the notion of "better" when it relies solely on human consensus. Human consensus can be politically motivated or biased.

Throughout history, powerful, learned men have come to consensus. They observed, they discussed, they practiced. They decided this or that was fact, this or that was better, and a standard was set. Brave others in the minority challenged the standard and discovered "better" or more accurate results. The standard changed to embrace that which was more sound, usually after much opposition from the majority. Scientific discovery is full of examples in that regard. Although science, unlike art, is regarded as intellectually knowable, both science and art utilize scientific inquiry – the science of comparison. Perception or how we see, becomes crucial to the process of observation.

Hume uses the analogy of being colorblind to explain why some critics do not see as others see. This reasoning assumes that "better" is more likely recognized by the many. Since the many establish the standard by consensus, and it is not easy to be in the minority, it might be to a man's disadvantage to hold opinions that would bar him from the "good taste" group. The colorblind theory assumes that group consensus is "better". I think it far more realistic to say that group consensus provides presumed shared agreement. Consensus alone does not always reveal what is really in the heart of a person. Consensus could merely indicate forced compliance. Consensus may be a result of intimidation or weakness. Hume's line of reasoning does allow for minority opinion, but consensus is valued more highly. Minority views will not achieve consensus even if they are true because art does not aim to be truthful. Hume does argue that while art does not aim to be truthful, it should aim to be "good". If good, then art can be "better" and ultimately "the best."

Hume says that there is no objective reality, but he uses the example of scientific inquiry, or the science of comparison, to explain how certainty in the standard is derived. He says that judgements of taste are necessarily subjective, but there is "but one truth", and the best of us find it and are able to describe it. In art, who decides what the truth is for all? What is "Truth in art"?

Hume argues that all sentiment and opinion is subjective, and that knowledge is merely sense perception. This might shatter the idea of society and order, but Hume speaks to that concern. He explains a basic principle of unification. He offers that consensus holds all the potentially ungovernable individuals together. People are held together by standards, by some generally accepted notion. We need these standards, at very least, to communicate efficiently – and at most to maintain order, even as we challenge ideas in the majority, and make room for new ideas and discoveries.

The remaining thought is this: that Hume acknowledges every person's right to sentiment and feeling. These feelings should not be governed, nor can they be. But for the sake of order in society and as the basis of a common reality, let us adopt standards. Let most of us agree. If we must have standards let them be set by people who will devote themselves to frequent observation and reflection.

Admittedly, some standards may change. In a broad sense, some standards *must* change to allow for advancement after new discoveries. However, in matters of art observation, Hume would insist that standards must remain constant. If art is one of the most personal expressions, should it be regulated by consensus? Can we accurately judge art if beauty is truly subjective?

Hume might say that art is not a question of truth but of consensus. Art is concerned with standards. Standards are necessarily better in the sense that they constitute the basis for informed opinion shared by the largest number of people – and for that reason only. Hume would say the standard is not more true, but it is "better". The concept of better, unlike sentiment, is not personal. Rather, it is shared. We must be thoughtful when we assign the term "better", as this judgment might be the product of persuasion and conformity rather than true consensus.

Hume provided an intellectual explanation of things rooted in the senses. Standards are, after all, group consensus that certain ideas are shared. When Hume suggested that good taste can be learned, he assumed that good taste, or better taste, was an absolute construct that could be measured and taught.

In art observation, the concept of "better" could be an indication of agreement rather than a confirmation of superiority of one judgement over another. I agree with Hume's argument that consensus sets the standard of taste. Majority opinion has that affect. I do not agree with Hume that the standard demonstrates superiority in judgment. Too often throughout history, men have been inspired toward consensus to ensure inclusion and acceptance. A desire to survive and be promoted among peers has unfortunately tainted the process of deep observation and commitment to truth. The concept of "better" in art observation remains an illusion. Like the notion of beauty, it is in the eye of the beholder.

A better building has certain aspects that must be achieved. The building must be architecturally sound (a strong foundation) etc. A building must meet specific codes to pass inspection. In this example, "better" is clear. As we examine art (a painting for example), can we apply the same process for design, construction, creating and observation of art? Who is the better artist? Who is the better observer of the art? Is the concept of "better" art too arbitrary; too subjective a notion to entangle with the delight and the practice of art observation? What is the better or best answer to this question?

If we center our arguments on art observation as a skill, what elements must be present to determine who is properly observing the art? Do art observation skills apply to all kinds of art?

Classical Rhetoric in the Modern Church:
A Study of Persuasive Communication

By: Elaine Patricia Walker

The Christian religion provides an enduring example of the power of persuasive discourse. Classical rhetoric is the foundation on which the church is built. Preachers and Priests rely on the substance of their argument and their ability to persuade. Regarding substance, the preacher has the advantage of building his or her message from historical fact. Jesus, on whom Christianity is based, was a citizen in the Mediterranean. He lived in the early first century of the Common Era (Crossan. xii). Jesus was born soon before 4 B.C.E. at Nazareth, a hamlet of about 200 people. He had at least six siblings. His people were the poorest of the Jews in the area (Johnson 4). Richard Weaver writes, "The Christian always had the story of Jesus…He could argue from fact, and this at once put him on grounds to persuade" (176).

In the modern church of the 21st century the focus is on persuasion. Persuasion is used to "win souls". Effective communication is crucial in Christianity. The ability to persuade determines the size of the church at large, and the number of faithful members of a local church, in particular. Not only is the modern church rooted in rhetoric, its future depends on it.

Weaver wrote concerning "modern rhetoric" and a decline in the acceptance of traditional Christianity. Weaver attributes the decline, in part, to the decline of acceptance of rhetoric. He writes that some in the modern scientific community are threatened by the idea of persuasion. These persons have invented a term, "psychological coercion" to express their fear. They are trying to re-label persuasion, assigning a negative context. I think that anyone with an opinion, including the reluctant scientist, engages in some form of persuasion when presenting an idea for acceptance. Opposition to rhetoric is not new. I discuss some of its opponents as well as those who defended it, in the body of this paper.

Classical Origins of Rhetoric

Rhetoric was practiced long before Christianity emerged. Stephen O'Leary and Brenda Brasher write "Rhetoric, conceived as the theory and practice of persuasive oratory, already had a long tradition when Christianity made its appearance on the intellectual and religious scene of the Roman Empire…Sophistic teachers conceived it as a practical art, the cultivation of which could lead human beings toward both power and virtue" (235).

Rhetoric evolved and was established in the fifth century B.C. (Poulakas. 3). In Athens during that time, every man considered to be educated had been taught rhetoric. It was this art that qualified a person for full participation in the democracy. "Certain Sophists [teachers of rhetoric] made the payment of their fees dependent upon some proof that they had actually given to a pupil the ability to persuade an audience" (Hunt. 22).

Rhetoric, with an emphasis on persuasion, was widely supported. O'Leary and Brasher explain the origins of rhetoric in the following passage:

> "The pre-Socratic Sophists, the earliest professors of the language arts, sought to train Greek citizens in the varieties of public speech necessary for participation in civic life...For Protagoras, rhetoric became a systematic method for the study and practice of controversy (dissoi logoi) ... Gorgias formed a rhetoric of flamboyant beauty as well as instrumental utility. Isocrates conceived of rhetoric as an essential skill in the practice of statecraft, and helped to shape an ideal conception of the citizen-orator which influenced later generations of Roman rhetoricians" (O'Leary and Brasher. 235).

Rhetoric also had passionate enemies. Plato was one of them. Everett Lee Hunt writes in *Historical Studies of Rhetoric and Rhetoricians* that Plato attacked rhetoric. Plato believed rhetoric was not an art. Hunt explains, "By an art, Plato meant more what we should call a science, a body of knowledge organized on universally valid principles" (40). Rhetoric's inclusion of learned persuasive technique was offensive to Plato.

Plato also rejected secular music, all fine and performing arts, and sports. He wrote that these are distractions and illusions that do not promote closeness to God.

Plato criticized Sophistic teaching and proposed what he called "true rhetoric", a religious rhetoric grounded in scientific knowledge of the human soul and its influences. Its purpose was to find a language that would impel the soul's motion toward God (O'Leary. 235). O'Leary and Brasher continue:

> "Plato's teachings greatly influenced many of the theologians of the early Christian era. Aristotle responded to Plato's attacks on rhetoric "by Reconstructing the conceptions of art, of knowledge and reason, and the ethical foundations of rhetoric." His Rhetoric "established the theoretical canons that remained in use for centuries…" Others who followed after Aristotle developed this potential with further theoretical contributions which became commonplaces of Hellenic rhetorical education: the division of rhetoric into the five canons of invention, arrangement, style, memory, and delivery…" (235).

Christianity was originally rejected by cultured Greeks and Romans. The immense power of the Roman Empire set itself against the growing sect, and within a short time, just claiming to be a Christian had become a capital offense (Visalli. 6). As Christianity expanded, it survived slander, threats, hatred and internal dissension, to gain power and respectability. After some 300 years it even won control of its onetime enemy, the Roman Empire.

The triumph of Christianity brought with it an awareness that a new or "modern" world, distinct from the ancient world, had come into being. The term *modern* comes from the writings of the sixth-century Christian statesman, Cassiodorus (Rattray.7). Christianity was to represent not only a break with the past but a means of transmitting the Greco-Roman heritage to later generations.

Christianity was rejected by Jews also. Most Jews thought about the coming Messiah in glorious terms. He would be a great king. He would overthrow oppression, destroy idolatry, establish justice, and bring peace. In place of such great expectations the disciples of Jesus proclaimed that a carpenter teacher from a small town, crucified by the Roman governor, was the Messiah.

To speak of the Messiah and crucifixion in the same breath seemed a contradiction during the time of Jesus, because the crucifixion was linked with disgrace during Roman rule. It implied that the crucified person was one who had so offended the laws of Rome as to deserve the most severe and demeaning punishment. Such a person could hardly be a savior. Or could he?

The disciples of Jesus were able to persuade audiences from all levels of society that the crucified Jesus was indeed a savior, the resurrected Messiah. In the book of Acts it is recorded that 3,000 people became disciples on one day, after hearing Simon Peter, one of Jesus' close friends. After Jesus' death, pilgrims and visitors from various regions were in town for the Pentecost celebration. Peter talked to them concerning Jesus in what must have been a very moving address. Persuasion has always been used in the Christian religion.

Christianity evolved from one of the most hated religions to the ruling religion of Rome. Force and punishment might have played a role in the early "acceptance" of Christianity, but how could such enduring change take place throughout history, if it were not for the powers of persuasion?

Jesus did not leave behind a single word of his own writing. He was known only through stories based on the disciples' memories (Visalli. 7). After his death, all that Jesus had done and said might have been forgotten if his followers had not begun to tell his story. But for decades the disciples wrote nothing down. For the first generations of Christians, Jesus' story was transmitted by word of mouth, first by his disciples who had known him personally, then by thousands of converts who retold the story.

Historical Uses of Rhetoric in the Christian Movement

Christians reported Jesus' words and actions for the purpose of winning converts and to instruct new believers. Their message was accepted, though much of what they said about Jesus was incredible. Some of the earlier hearers of the disciples' exhortations knew Jesus socially or they had heard of the miraculous healings he performed near their hometowns. But most of the new Christians accepted Jesus as the Messiah because they were persuaded by words.

Rhetorical form was implicit in the oral tradition of early Christianity. The stories about Jesus would not have been as effective without persuasion in the delivery. As Christianity spread from Jerusalem, we can gather that persuasion was the driving force that propelled the movement and caused thousands to ponder, and then accept this new doctrine.

The Christian movement met with great opposition. For example, there was Saul, a strict Pharisee, who quickly became one of the most notorious persecutors of early Christians. Saul was a native of the Greek city of Tarsus in Cilicia, near the southern coast of present-day Turkey (Visalli. 39). Saul also had a Greco-Roman name: Paul. Paul's writings show that he was educated both in the current philosophy of the Greek and Roman world and in the traditions of the Hebrew Scriptures and their interpretations among the Jews. From his father he had inherited Roman citizenship. Paul was a Jew first, committed to the way of life of the Pharisees. Paul was reared to be devoted to the law of the God of Israel, not that of Rome (Visalli. 41). When some followers of Jesus, considered to be no more than a sect at the time, argued that the law and the Temple were important, but the physical temple was no longer central, they struck at the heart of all that Paul believed. Paul was as far from the followers of Jesus as it was possible to be.

After what Paul described as a spiritual experience during his travels toward Damascus to punish more Christians, he was "supernaturally" persuaded to accept Christianity. Paul reports that he heard the voice of the crucified Jesus. His traveling companions were witnesses. To the amazement of many, Paul forsook all to preach about Jesus. He became chief advocate of

Christianity to Rome and the surrounding areas. His advocacy eventually reached the whole world.

Paul was familiar with rhetoric through his education. He utilized rhetoric as he persuaded the urban educated classes of Rome and Antioch to consider Christianity. He became one of the most well-known authorities on Christian doctrine. To validate and popularize Christianity in Rome, he used methods and terms that his Roman audiences found familiar and acceptable (Weber. 193).

Historical writings confirm that rhetoric was part of the culture of Rome's educated class. It is this audience that Paul initially addressed with his concept of Christianity. Stephen O'Leary and Brenda Brasher write: "Paul's address in Acts…the speech on the "Unknown God" is an astute adaptation of the Christian message to the understanding of an educated urban audience…" (235). Paul had to use his training in rhetoric to be heard by his audience, and to be convincing. "…The earliest audiences for Christian preaching were largely composed of Hellenized Jews. Many among these audiences were likely to have had training in the gymnasia that existed in most large cities of the Empire, an experience that naturally would have exposed them to rhetoric as part of their ordinary instructional curriculum" (Kinneavy. 56).

Paul offers proof that rhetoric was used in Christianity during the early years. O'Leary and Brasher write, "Whether as oral preaching or as written text…the success of the Christian message can be traced directly to the efforts of earliest Christians to find a hearing in the ancient forum by adapting the rhetorical forms and methods that prevailed there, and to transform these forms and methods for their own uses." (239).

Many great theologians of old were trained in rhetorical schools, for example: Augustine, Basil of Caesarea, Lactantius (O'Leary. 239). Some who received training in rhetoric condemned it after their conversion to Christianity. Nevertheless, rhetoric and its influences prevailed.

St. Augustine was an accomplished teacher of rhetoric who later embraced Christianity. His *On Christian Doctrine (De Doctrina Christiana)* contains Augustine's advice to preachers on how to interpret the scriptures. He explained that they should learn the art of rhetoric in order to equip themselves to instruct and strengthen the faith of their audiences. In his work, he justifies the use of rhetoric by the Christian preacher. In the conclusion of *On Christian Doctrine*, St. Augustine tells how the preacher should adapt his style to both his aim and his audience. (Masten, et al. viii).

Contemporary Application

With basic rhetorical principles of persuasion, the modern church has consistently presented well-drafted, solid arguments. Henry Chadwick writes of the Christian church, "…the church could not escape reasoned argument if it was ever to explain itself and so extend its mission to the world" (9). The modern church is faced with the challenges that sophisticated, educated audiences bring. Just as Paul realized that it was necessary to speak intelligently about Jesus, about the resurrection, and about salvation through faith to his audiences of educated people, the modern preacher approaches his audience with similar thoughtfulness. It is important to note here that the modern Pentecostal preacher is preaching Paul's messages. Paul's educational influences were weaved into his messages; therefore, rhetoric is inextricably mingled with the sermons we hear today. Much of the content for today's sermons are taken from Paul's letters and other writings recorded about his Christian journey. The message is thousands of years old, but it is relevant and effective today. Modern preachers proclaiming Jesus as the Christ have continued to use the rhetorical principles, following Paul's example.

The Pentecostal church thrived worldwide from the 1990's to around 2016. Large congregations in Africa, Asia, and America grew by the thousands during those years. Effective use of persuasion (rhetoric) was a big part of the reason for that growth.

Rhetoric, persuasive oratory, accounted for at least 90% of the influx of new members to the Christian church. The church has long ago recognized that knowledge of the bible as well as attention to social and cultural dynamics are important as it recruits and serves a diverse, growing membership. Today's Pentecostal church has parallel concerns to Paul, who set the precedent for evangelism.

Honorable "preachers" persuade people to love God and one another, to be responsible citizens, to contribute positively to communities, and to drive social change for the good of all people. Plato, who seemed concerned about spirituality and virtue, would support the modern church in that it encourages men to seek God above all things, and to work for the betterment of society through service and ethical leadership.

The modern church uses rhetoric/persuasion in very beneficial ways. People have been persuaded not to commit suicide. Young married couples have been persuaded to pray and work through their problems together and as a result of this, they renewed their commitment to God and to each other. Substance abusers have been persuaded to try sobriety and have been helped by the church. Persuasion is a good tool when it is used in positive ways.

The faith that Jesus elicited in his first disciples caused them to launch one of the most significant historical movements; the birth and eventual spread of Christianity. Persuasive oratory was the means by which the story of

Jesus was spread. What other force could so captivate the attention of staunch persecutors, like Saul, and win them to the causes of Christ? Acts 17:2-4 states:

> "And Paul, as his manner was, went in unto them, and three sabbath days reasoned with them out of the scriptures, explaining that Christ had to suffer and he rose from the dead, and saying this Jesus, whom I preach unto you, is Christ. And some of them believed, and consorted with Paul and Silas; and of the devout Greeks a great multitude…" (Holy Bible, The New Testament).

In the Preface of the book *Readings in Classical Rhetoric*, edited by Patricia Masten, Phillip Rollinson and Marion Sousa, these words are written: "Christians can use rhetoric for their own education and in sermons" (vii). The editors were referring to Basil and Augustine's suggestions for the use of rhetoric. Rhetoric laid the foundation for Christian oratory, and it is largely responsible for its widespread growth throughout the modern world over the past centuries.

The modern Pentecostal church knows that people who are on destructive paths might not chose a different way which leads to life and purpose, except they be persuaded to do so.

-End-

References

Chadwick, H. 1996. Early Thought and the Classical Tradition. New York. Oxford University Press

Crossan, J.D. 1994. Jesus. New York. Harper Collins.

Hunt, E.L. 1961. Historical Studies of Rhetoric and Rhetoricians. New York. Cornell University Press.

Jaeger, w. 1936. The Theology of the Early Greek Philosophers. Oxford. Clarendon Press

Johnson, J.T. 1985. Scripture and Society: From Reform in the Old World to Revival in the New. Philadelphia. Fortress Press.

Johnson, T.L. 1996. The Real Jesus. New York. Harper Collins.

Kennedy, G.A. 1991. On Rhetoric. New York. Oxford University Press.

Kennedy, G.A. 1963. The Art of Persuasion. Princeton University Press.

Kinneavey, J. 1987. Greek Rhetorical Origins of Christian Faith. New York. Oxford University Press.

Masten, P. 1990. Readings from Classical Rhetoric. Illinois. Southern Illinois University Press.

O'Leary, S. and Brasher, B. 1996 Religious Communication from the Ancient Agora to the Virtual Form: Christianity and the Tradition of Classical Rhetoric. Albany. State University of New York Press.

Populakos, J. 1991. The Possibility of Rhetoric's Early Beginnings, Evanston. Northwestern University Press.

Weaver, R.M. 1970. Language is Sermonic: The Cultural Role of Rhetoric. Baten Rouge. Louisiana State University Press

Discovering Connections in Education and Brain Sciences

Elaine Patricia Walker, Ed.D.

How will educators, researchers, and neuroscientists effectively share our knowledge of the brain and learning? In the 21st Century, the assertion is that teachers, researchers in education, and cognitive neuroscientists will have increasingly important information to offer regarding how brains learn and thrive. Fortunately, we are discussing our questions and findings at conferences, in print, and while we develop our active research.

In the year 2021, although less is known about the living/learning brain than any other organ of the human body, recent technological advances are enabling brain researchers to examine and engage the living brain in exciting ways. Broader uses of imaging technologies are beginning to provide unparalleled insight into brain function. A global emphasis on human potential fuels our growing interest in the brain. Are we learning more efficiently as we rely more heavily on technologies? What are teachers observing about brains in their classrooms?

Many of our best teachers have great interest in the brain, particularly in how the brain learns. Educators have worked tirelessly to engage and challenge the brains in their care. Investigation by brain researchers could provide empirical data for what practitioners in learning environments have proposed:

Field of Education	Neuroscience
1. Brains that are challenged in a nurturing learning environment are more likely to accurately interpret and retain key information and remain engaged for larger periods of time. (Jensen, E.)	1. Brain scans of children who were introduced to information and concepts, in an enriched environment, showed remarkable dendrite growth (positive changes in structural activity) and frequent processing activity associated with higher uses of glucose and oxygen. (Diamond, M., & Hopson, J.)
2. No two students are exactly alike. Learner individuality should be considered in the design and execution of lesson plans. Instruction should accommodate different learning styles. (Caine, G., & Caine, R.N.)	2. Brains within the same age group receive and process data at different rates. (Eisenberg, L.) No two brains are exactly alike. (Greenfield, S.A.)
3. Experience shapes the brain. Activities and experiences in the classroom can impact brain development. (Sylwester, R.)	3. Learning experiences change and reorganize the brain's structure and physiology. (Diamond, M.)
4. Students learn from reading and hearing, but activities such as performing and experimenting are very important for effective learning and retention. (Towse, J.N., Hitch, G.J., & Hutton, U.)	4. The most lasting changes in the brain occur when a student performs an experiment compared to when a student reads about an experiment someone else conducted. (Jacobs, B., Schall, M., & Scheibel, A.B.)

5. Multi-modal instruction increases likelihood that students will recall information (hearing, seeing, touching, discussing, and experimenting.) (Sousa, D.)	5. When an experience enters the brain, it is deconstructed and distributed all over the cortex. The emotional content is stored in the amygdala, visual images in the occipital lobes, source memory in the frontal lobes and where you were learning is stored in the parietal lobes. When you recall information, you have to reconstruct it. Since memories are reconstructed, the more ways students have the information represented in the brain, the more pathways they have for reconstructing, thus the richer the memory. (Lasley, E.)
6. Emotion and passion can be a primary catalyst in the learning process. Teachers can help students to enjoy learning by inspiring passion for, and emotional investment in, assignments, topics, or activities. (Wolfe, P., & Kovakik, R.)	6. Two structures deep within each hemisphere of the brain, called the amygdala, regulate our emotional responses which have the ability to either impede or enhance learning. Too much negative arousal (such as situations that contain elements that a person perceives to be threatening) can cause emotion to be dominant over cognition. The rational/thinking part of the brain is less efficient when a person feels threatened. The environment must be challenging but physically and psychologically safe for learning to occur. (LeDoux, J.) Emotional experiences increase likelihood for recall. Those experiences linked to strong emotion are more vivid and will be remembered longer than experiences void of strong emotional links or content. (Cahill, L.)

The noble search to unlock the mysteries of the human brain and the subsequent possibilities for application of scientific findings to classroom practice may well be accelerated by a joining of forces. What more can be discovered as educators and scientists devote constructive energies and shared passion to the acquisition of new knowledge of the brain?

More effort is necessary in educational and scientific research communities, to refrain from ridicule of the pace and the processes of discovery. Scientists and educators use different methods and measures to observe behaviors, and to gather data that suggests or documents brain function and brain activity. We can benefit from more joint investigation in the ongoing search for facts about how the healthy brain functions and learns. When discussion outpaces debate concerning the usefulness of brain research in classroom practice – the exploration of the untried will likely lead to more relevant discoveries.

John T. Bruer, president of the James S. McDonnell Foundation in St. Louis, Missouri insists that brain research, through the late 1990s, offered nothing that should encourage the modification of educational approaches in the classroom. Bruer argued that much of what teachers and brain enthusiasts attributed to new brain research findings is actually based on a cognitive and constructivist model of learning that is rooted in more than 30 years of psychological research. Progressive education reforms, "learning environments low in threat and high in challenge", for example, "can be found in any current textbook on educational psychology. None of the evidence comes from brain research", says Bruer. (In Search of Brain-Based Education, *Phi Delta Kappan*, 180 (9):649, May 1999). Bruer asks, "Where does the science end and the speculation begin?", suggesting that teachers especially are guilty of 1.) trying new ideas for which science data does not exist, or 2.) incorrectly applying brain related information in their practice. Bruer offers this note of caution to teachers: "Thoroughly examine neuroscience literature before applying any new techniques to classroom practice."

Some for-profit sales-driven companies claim that they offer products that are "brain-based". I encourage instructors to rely on the science and the "proven," not on commercialism and hype. In this, I agree with Bruer's sentiment. I am not criticizing or promoting any "product". Rather, my intent is to encourage collaboration across disciplines that focus on the learning brain.

For the teacher:

How the brain learns, the structure and function of the human brain, and environmental factors that impact the brain's ability to process and recall – all of these considerations are important. Teachers share the crucial responsibility to inspire brains in the learning environment, therefore, a basic understanding of the anatomy and developmental function of the brain can be quite useful. I certainly support the inclusion of brain studies in teacher preparation and continuing education.

Scientists cannot tell us all there is to know about the human brain. We simply do not know, yet, everything about the life of the brain. We need not wait until all the data is in to try new approaches in the learning environment. All the data may never be available in our lifetime. We know enough today to understand that the learning process is complex and that learners gain understanding in different ways. Teachers have, through their practice for centuries, done amazing work with learners. Later, science explains the outcomes and enriches our action research in education with important information.

Teachers did not wait for scientific data to prove that a child who prefers a variety of learning approaches will remember more vocabulary words if the child can sing the words, associate the words with images, write the words, and find the words in a word "treasure hunt" around the classroom. But this combination of strategies works very well with the child. The teacher had no scientific data that proved that the child who likes to jump will be better at addition and subtraction by jumping in a "math hopping grid", as the child learns mathematical computation. But that child's math scores increased using this learning strategy. The teacher combined play with serious work and her student thrived. There is a scientific explanation for what happened in the learners' brains. Cognitive neuroscience provides some answers. Might teaching be enhanced by scientifically corroborated data? Should we reconsider "The Science of Teaching?" as well as the science of learning? Can we work together?

I advocate for dialogue across the educational and scientific research communities. Educators can learn from neuroscientists and neuroscientists can learn from educators. Our future language and efforts can reflect unity across disciplines. Progress in brain studies demands cooperation, shared resources, open communication. In our work, let's continue to discover the connections in the fields of education and brain sciences. Engaging the human brain, stimulating the mind is an adventure! This adventure encompasses the classroom, the laboratory, and other research environments.

It is true that teachers spend hours at a time each weekday with a classroom full of brains. Surely teachers should be included in the discussions about how the brain learns. Even the neuroscientist learned from a teacher before she became a scientist of the brain. Both disciplines can advance the human experience: Cognitive Neuroscience <u>and</u> classroom practice. The future of education will be shaped by how well we utilize these connections.

Publications:
Journal of Developmental Education
Review of Educational Research
Journal of Teacher Education

Conferences:
The Learning Brain

About the Presenter:
Elaine Patricia Walker is a Doctor of Education and Researcher.

References

Bruer, J.T. (1997, May). In Search of Brain Based Education. Bloomington, IN: *Phi Delta Kappan, 180(9): 649.*

Cahill, L. (2000, January). *Emotions and Memory.* Speech. San Diego, CA. The Learning Brain Expo.

Caine, G., & Caine, R.N. (1997). *Education on the edge of possibility.* Alexandria, VA: ASCD.

Diamond, M., & Hopson, J. (1998). *Magic trees of the mind.* New York: Dutton Books, (1999) Penguin-Putnam Group.

Eisenberg, L. (1995, November). The social construction of the human brain. *American Journal of Psychiatry* 152, 1563-1575

Greenfield, S.A. (1997). *The human brain: A guided tour.* New York: Basic Books/Harper Collins.

Jacobs, B., Schall, M., & Scheibel, A.B. (1993). A quantitative dendritic analysis of Wernicke's area in humans: Gender, hemispheric and environmental factors. *Journal of Comparative Neurology 327 (1)*, 97-111.

Jensen, E. (1998). *Teaching with the brain in mind.* Alexandria, VA: ASCD

Kotulak, R. (1996). *Inside the brain: Revolutionary discoveries of how the mind works.* Kansas City: Andrews McMeel

Lasley, E. (1997). *How the brain learns and remembers.* Brainwork 7, 1-9.

LeDoux, J. (1996). *The emotional brain.* New York: Simon & Schuster.

Sabbatini, R.M.E. (1997, August/September). EEG Brain mapping, *Brain and Mind Magazine.* A publication of Campinas Medical School, Brazil.

Sousa, D. (1999). *How the brain learns.* Alexandria, VA. ASCA.

Sylwester, R. (1995). *A celebration of neurons: An educator's guide to the brain.* Alexandria, UA: Association for Supervision and Curriculum Development.

Towse, J.N., Hitch, G.J., & Hutton, U. (1998. August). A reevaluation of working memory capacity in children. *Journal of Memory and Language, 39 (2),* 195-217.

Wolfe, P., & Kovakik, R. (2001). *Brain matters.* Alexandria, VA: ASCD.

Lysistrata: A play by Aristophanes

An analysis
by Elaine Patricia Walker

Aristophanes gave to Greece, to the world, over forty dramas. Through these theatrical works, he provided insight into the cultural and political climate of his time. *Lysistrata* is his most popular comedy. We should take note of this. What message was so profound that the play became his most performed work? The play continued to be presented hundreds of years after it was written.

Lysistrata focused on political and social conflict, women's rights, war strategy, abuse of power, and social order. These are powerful themes. These topics continue to drive dialogue into the 21st century.

Using the language of comedy and metaphor the playwright conveys very serious concerns. The use of comedy was a shrewd choice. As in Aristophanes' day, comedy is still used effectively to relay discontent. Consider the modern-day comics criticizing the President or expressing outrage about war, for example. Aristophanes used comedy to get his message out to the broadest audience. With the ravages of war all around, comedy may have been a welcome outlet. Comedy was utilized as an effective way to emphasize the need for a united community, to make a strong political statement, and to diffuse more serious conflict. The theatrical stage served as a sort of pulpit, enforcing moral values, social consciousness, and public responsibility.

In the play, Aristophanes used the dynamics of relationships to illustrate his main point (relationships as the core of human co-existence/community). The characters are in conflict. The women want the war to end. They refuse to have sex with the men until the war is settled. The women are upset that their opinions and advice are disregarded. They feel victimized. Issues of respect and equality are evident. Debate prevails about power and politics in the home and in government. A war of the sexes, perhaps? Only on the surface. There is more here.

Lysistrata may well represent Sparta, the enemy. The Commissioner, distraught, his authority threatened, may represent Athens. The fierce dialogue between the characters represents the fighting that goes on in the heat of the battle. Both opponents use deadly force, represented by the weapon of the tongue. The characters are citizens of the same city, but they are at odds with one another. Through this, Aristophanes indicates the threat of internal revolt, the escalation of citizen discontent. The play also conveys a call to leadership to reorganize (note the example of Lysistrata's story about weaving, Perry, p. 72). Athens could learn from their enemy, but they were too stubborn and unyielding. They lost the war.

Finally, "Lysistrata" is a lesson about the wars we fight in life. Aristophanes cleverly disguises "wisdom for survival" in war metaphor and comedy. He shows us ourselves, at war in our homes and with our neighbors. Perhaps the battles fought among neighbors never end in real victory. And if war is useful at all, it serves only one purpose: to teach men the virtues of peace.

-END-

Bibliography

Moultan, Carroll. "Aristophanes." Ancient Writers of Greece and Rome. Volume
    I. 1982

Perry, Marvin. "Lysistrata." Sources of the Western Tradition, third edition. Ed.
    S.W. Wakley. Houghton Mifflin Company, 1995. Chapter 3:8, 69-73.

Notes:
- White Paper/Theatre

Topics:
- Social Justice
- Social Reflection
- Script Analysis

The Role of Nature and Nurture in the Learning Experience

By Elaine Patricia Walker, Ed.D.

Introduction

Some researchers argue that as a determinant for human development, heredity (genetics) plays a far greater role than does one's environment after birth. Others insist that cultural experiences are the dominant factors in human development. The argument has graduated from a "One or the other" as the sole factor of influence (i.e., Plato and Descartes vs. the Empiricists) to a "Which force is greater?" argument (i.e., Locke vs. Rowe).

For this discussion, the field of developmental psychology informs how we interpret the definition of the terms "Nature" (biological inheritance) and "Nurture" (cultural and external environmental influences). "The nature verses nurture debate involves the extent to which particular aspects of behavior are a product of either inherited or acquired influences" (Hernandez, L.M., Blazer, D.G., 2006). The discussion remains important in the year 2020. It is possible that the topic and its implications are more important than when the debate first began thousands of years ago. Scientific advances and current practices encourage a closer look at the topic.

Nature and nurture frame behavior in the human experience. These two influences can help educators and education researchers to understand and design experiences for our learners, helping us to decide what programs and efforts might assist students in learning environments. Should practitioners build in nurturing elements or presume limits based on "nature" and the predispositions imposed with that position? Are either "nature" or "nurture" significant enough influencers to warrant any modification to how we teach and guide learning experiences?

Overview

I will briefly examine the history of the argument, how the argument has developed over time, and current positions as we proceed through the 21st Century. I will discuss the implication for taking a position on either side of the argument. I will state my position on the subject "Nature vs. Nurture," as it relates to human behavior in learning environments. My interest in the topic persists as an education researcher and practitioner. Finally, I offer future considerations and key questions.

The History of the Argument

Historically, the principle of the "Nature / Nurture" argument can be traced to Plato, the philosopher who believed that at least some ideas were innate. Human development would then be governed by a pattern "built-in" at birth. Later, French philosopher Rene Descartes held a similar position in which he argued that the development of ideas was independent of physical circumstance. These early philosophers provided an arena for debate on concepts such as thought and being, beauty, and indirectly on the subject of human development. Their influence can be seen in modern researchers, such as D.C. Rowe (1994). Rowe argues that "Developmental Psychologists have greatly exaggerated the effects of 'nurture' on variation in personality, intelligence, and other characteristics and greatly underestimated the effects of heredity." Rowe claims, as Plato might have, that personality and intelligence are governed by nature, and only mildly influenced by "nurture".

British philosopher John Locke, (an Empiricist), argued that all knowledge is created by experience. Psychologists B.F. Skinner and John Watson agreed with Locke's assumption that, "at birth the mind is a blank slate, in Latin a *tabula rasa*" (Skinner, 1957). These researchers represent the "nurture" side of the argument, citing experience after birth as the governing determinant for human development.

The argument, as it continues, acknowledges the presence of both biological and cultural influences on human development, but the disagreement persists concerning the extent to which these factors determine development. The question, "Which of the factors is most important?", drives the current research. Psychologist Helen Bee, author of The Growing Child (1995), writes:

> "Both nature and nurture, biology and culture, are involved in all aspects of development, although there has been long-standing disagreement on the relative importance of these factors. Current thinking about the "nature" side of the equation emphasizes not only the role of maturation but also points to potential inborn strategies of perceiving or responding to the environment... Current thinking about the "nurture" side...emphasizes... the importance of examining the entire ecological system in which development occurs, including culture" (27).

Researchers on both sides of the argument today provide evidence that heredity (in-born) and culture (external influence) contribute to human development. The study of genetic contributions to individual behavior, called behavior genetics, has yielded data that suggests heredity affects such things as cognitive ability (IQ), personality, characteristics and even certain behaviors (i.e., pathological behavior). This kind of genetic research is featured in many arguments supporting "nature" as the more important factor in development. The concept of "inborn biases" or "constraints" on development is a popular notion similar in principle to Descartes' notion of inborn ideas (Slobin, 1985). Modern psychologists argue that babies are "programmed" by genetics to respond in particular ways, therefore genetics, in this argument, plays the dominant role in human development.

On the other side of the argument, researcher Richard Aslin (1981) provides an analysis of the potential impact of environment on development in his "Five models of possible relationship between maturation and environment". Essentially, Aslin supports the idea that nurture is the dominant force in development. Child development specialist E. Thelen author of Development as a Dynamic System (1992), also underscores the crucial role of environment on a child's development.

The question of "degree of importance" has not been definitively answered.

Implications for Choosing a Side

The nature side of the argument in the 1990s emphasized the role of genetics/heredity (Thelen & Adolph, 1992). Human thoughts and behaviors can be perceived as inevitable (pre-determined) but alterable (via scientific intervention through DNA manipulation, for example). Those who choose

91

this nature argument do not assign greatest importance to external human environments (family, social experiences) as significantly dominant forces in development. Theorists who argue that nature is the driving force for development might point out that "children with different inborn qualities, such as vulnerability or resilience, may be affected differently by the same environment" (Bee. p. 27). Here, it is the inborn quality, not the environment, that ultimately determines development and explains behavior.

In the year 2020, and presumably beyond, advances in scientific research enable the design of human characteristics such as eye color and other physical features. Genome manipulation can prevent disease. Scientists can clone humans and influence human behavior and learning abilities. Natural biological development can be replaced by genetic manipulation. Choosing a "Nature" position will be more complicated as the genetic design options become available to consumers. How will this science impact the field of Education?

The nurture side of the argument emphasizes experiences "after birth" as most important to the development process. Those who choose this argument may acknowledge heredity as a factor in development, but they do not identify heredity as the governing force in human development. They might argue that genetics' greatest influence is on physical characteristics such as height or weight. They might allow that heredity could trigger some behavioral patterns, such as pathological behaviors. However, nurture theorists argue that all behaviors are subject to change in physical environments where social factors dictate or strongly influence development (Thelen, 1992). What kinds of activities should educators include in a nurture-driven learning environment?

My Position

I agree with Helen Bee who says a child's development is a product of some interaction of nature and nurture: "No aspect of development is entirely one or the other" (p. 3). I am convinced that nature plays a significant role in human development. Genetic codes reveal complex but definite patterns that dictate human tendencies, physical attributes, behaviors, and some would argue, even human potential in certain areas. While genetics cannot be ignored as an important factor, environmental experiences, after birth, can profoundly influence behavior. Tendencies can be redirected, and potential can be heightened by the presence of nurturing caregivers, a loving environment, and an appropriate attention to deficits. I think that future medical and social scientific research will lead to new discoveries that will provide additional insight. Both factors, heredity and environment (nativism and empiricism) will prove equally important at different stages in the human experience, particularly as we consider learning and teaching.

Future Considerations (Global)

As we become increasingly global, researchers may be drawn to examine "nurture" in multi-cultural and cross-cultural situations, which could cause a shift in our focus and conclusions. Medical and genetic research is advancing rapidly, faster than ever before in human history. As people all over the world interact more often, I trust that we will learn more about our developmental similarities and differences through combined efforts in social studies and joint scientific research. Perhaps the focus will shift from "Which is most important: Nature or Nurture" to "Why are both important, and how can we apply principles from both influences to help learners throughout the world?"

Future Considerations (Increase in Health Concerns)

Education Professionals, Behavioral Specialists, Psychologists and Medical Doctors report increases in cases of unhealthy anxiety, attention deficits, depression, and other severe challenges that negatively impact learners. From the late 1980's to the year 2020, millions of school aged students (K-12, college/post-secondary, and graduate level) reported crippling anxiety that decreases their ability to do their best work and to enjoy life and learning.

Can researchers conclude that today's learners have in-born biological conditions that have made them susceptible to psychological (mental and emotional) vulnerability? Or, are the alarming numbers of today's compromised learners a result of a "nurture" issue? Not enough or not the right application? Too much?

Key Questions

1. To the extent that nature plays its role in human development and behavior, what can Education Professionals do to get the most out of the science embedded in this reality? If learners come into classrooms, and other learning environments, "pre-wired," how do educators use this "knowing" to benefit all in the learning environment?

2. When should educators/teachers/coaches/parents address "nurture" as they interact with learners? Is applying "nurture" a science or an art? Is there a correct way to "nurture" a learner?

3. Are there other factors that contribute to the high-anxiety and behavioral pathologies that we contend with in the 21st Century classroom? Can we trace human behavior and learning behaviors to distinctly nature or nurture causes?

4. Should we broaden our discussion to include Post Traumatic Stress Disorders (PTSD) that indicate shared stress (global, communal, familial)?

5. If "nature" (heredity) is a key factor, do we look to the parents of learners for clues that can predict behavior?

6. What other questions should educators explore?

References

Aslin, R.N. (1981). <u>Development of perception</u>. Psychological perspectives. Vol. 2, pp 45-93. New York: Academic Press.

Bee, H. (1995). <u>The growing child</u>. New York, NY: Harper Collins College Publishers.

Hernandez, Lyla M. and Blazer, Dan G. Eds. (2006). <u>Genes, Behavior, and the Social Environment, Moving Beyond the Nature/Nurture Debate</u>. By the Institute of Medicine, Board on Health Sciences Policy, Committee on Assessing Interactions Among Social, Behavioral, and Genetic Factors in Health.

Morrison, F.J., Alberts, D.M. & Griffin, E.M. (1997). <u>Nature-Nurture in the classroom.</u> Developmental Psychology, 33 (2), pp. 254-262.

Rowe, D.C. (1994). <u>The limits of experience: Genes, experience, and behavior</u>. New York, NY: Guilford Press.

Skinner, B.F. (1952). <u>Verbal behavior</u>. New York, NY: Prentice-Hall.

Thelen, E (1992). <u>Development as a dynamic system</u>. Current directions in psychological science, 1. pp 189-193

Walker, S. and Plomin, R. (2007). <u>The Nature – Nurture Question:</u> Teacher's perceptions of how genes and the environment influence educationally relevant behavior. (pp. 509-516).

Practicing Moral Leadership in Higher Education

Pulitzer Prize winner and leadership studies expert James MacGregor Burns wrote, "Moral leadership is not mere preaching, or the uttering of pieties, or the insistence on social conformity. Moral leadership emerges from, and always returns to, the fundamental wants and needs, aspirations, and values of the followers" (Wren. Chapter 61, p. 483). Burns argues that the authentic needs of the followers must be addressed to achieve moral leadership. He concludes that The Golden Rule (Do unto others as you would have them do unto you) is "inadequate" because, he says, "it measures the wants and needs of others simply by our own". The idea here is to do unto others according to their preferences, and not as we might like. Part of the process of moral leadership is finding out what followers want, what they have determined are their collective needs, what their values are. For Burns, a moral leader's focus remains on the followers.

Author J. Thomas Wren commits only one paragraph to Burns' treatment of Moral Leadership in his book The Leader's Companion (p. 483). This paragraph is an excerpt from Burns' book Leadership (1978). Burns' book was written more than 40 years ago. His references to morality in leadership are echoed in writings that date as far back as 2,000 years. According to Burns, advocating morality in leadership is not "mere preaching". His golden rule reference (a biblical passage in the Christian Bible, Book of Matthew, Chapter 7, Verse 12) draws our attention to one of history's most studied role models for moral leadership and followship: Jesus of Nazareth, the religious historical figure of the early first century of the common era. Jesus insisted that followship and service are important foundations for real leadership, and that the greatest leaders are the greatest servants. Moral leadership is rooted in service to followers. This philosophy persists in the 21st century organization.

In this writing, I examine the institution of higher education. I agree that moral leadership must remain the goal in higher education in the development of moral leaders in every discipline, in every area of study. Moral leadership grounds our passing on of knowledge, information, and ideas.

Dr. Howard T. Prince II, former Dean of the School of Leadership Studies at the University of Richmond and currently a Dean at the University of Texas in Austin, is the author featured in Wren's second chapter on Moral Leadership (Chapter 62). Prince writes from the perspective of a leader's ability to influence moral development in others. Prince examines the three major theories of Moral Development which are Sigmund Freud's Psychoanalytic Approach, Lawrence Kohlberg's Cognitive Approach, and Albert Bandura's Social Learning Approach to Moral Development. Of these three approaches, Prince cites Bandura's theory as the most practical and applicable for today's organizational leader.

Freud claimed that moral development peaked very early in a child's life. If this assumption were correct, morality and behaviors that indicate moral consideration would be locked in, almost fully developed by age 6. The implications for the organizational leader using Freud's argument are that there is little to nothing a leader can do to influence positive moral development in adults, scholars, or workers because people have already achieved moral maturity in early childhood. By the time they are adults, they are not likely to change or be influenced. In this example, the leader cannot influence behaviors. The organizational leader is restricted to selecting scholars, workers and/or colleagues who are self-governed and presumed likely to practice moral behaviors without role models, encouragement, or reward.

Prince argues that Freud's theory is not well supported by independent evidence. He says, "The lack of research support for the implication that moral development occurs very early in life is important to the organizational leader. If moral development is instead a continuing process, then the leader may be able to foster moral development among organizational members" (486).

Kohlberg's theory is that moral development occurs in stages, over time. The development is interpreted as initially primitive, based on avoiding punishment, then centered on self-interest. The next stage occurs when the person considers relationships with others as important in moral reasoning. The lower level of development associates a desire for approval from others when making moral decisions. A higher level of development demonstrates consideration of the viewpoints of others, a sense of duty to a social system, and a determination to do what is in the interest of all involved. The highest stage of development is Level 3, Stage 6, in which a person practices consistent moral principles and has respect for the dignity of all people regardless of specific laws or rules. Kohlberg argues, "this sequence is fixed and develops over time from one state to the next as our capacity for moral reasoning increases".

Kohlberg's theory identifies intelligence as a key factor for developing highest-stage moral development. He argues that moral behavior is secondary to the moral reasoning process. According to

Kohlberg, it is the "thought process" behind moral behavior which determines whether the person is moral rather than the behavior itself (488).

If the thought process is key, then we must consider how the thought process is developed. External influences may play a significant role. It is important how a person is treated and spoken to, whether they are encouraged to try, encouraged to think, encouraged to learn. If a person is rewarded for demonstrating behaviors that appear moral, then it is easier to make moral decisions. Constructive responses from others help to shape critical thinking and reasoning processes. Kohlberg's theory can be applied in the workplace. Leaders within organizations can expect to influence moral behaviors of workers by offering positive feedback, modeling desired behaviors, rewarding, and including workers in moral decision-making activities.

Bandura's Social Learning Approach emphasizes conditioning and imitation (reward/punishment and modeling). Wren has determined that Bandura's theory has the strongest application for today's organizational leaders. This theory has been the most well-supported by research. Using Bandura's theory, "leaders can influence the moral conduct of others by demonstrating the desired behavior, rewarding ethical behavior and discouraging the unethical conduct" (489).

Summary

James MacGregor Burns emphasizes the importance of considering the needs of others, as they define their needs. He insists that moral leadership is first and foremost about the followers. Leaders who practice true moral leadership do so when they respect the values and desires of their followers.

Howard T. Prince II writes about the thought process associated with behaviors that appear to be moral. He is more concerned with why a person decides to do what appears to be right. He claims that people gradually move through stages of moral development and that the act is secondary to the motive for the act. The more a person matures along the developmental stages, the more likely it becomes that the person will decide to select moral actions based on genuine concern for others and uncompromising commitment to justice.

As we lead organizations and units, the most important aspect of the discussion regarding moral leadership is that the dialogue may help leaders to practice morality in our organizations, and in greater society. If the discussion can help to inspire moral action in the workplace, on our campuses, and in our communities, then the theories and the subsequent examination of those theories is well worth academic attention. An examination of what moral leadership is not (for example, Burn's argument that it is not "mere preaching") and a theoretical comparison of moral development (Prince's comparison of three theories) would be useless without the intent to practice morality, in the home, in communities, in the workplace, and in our schools.

As we begin the year 2022, America is facing a moral leadership crisis. Moral leaders are sorely needed. Without a commitment to moral leadership, how will the country progress? How will organizations and communities thrive? Practicing moral leadership may well be the deciding factor for the quality of life within our organizations and our world.

-END-

Social Judgment Theory

Considerations for Communication Strategists

by Elaine Patricia Walker

Introduction

Your message might make a positive, necessary, or profitable difference. How do you get people to be open to what you have to say? How can you know the best approach to use in reaching a group with your message? If you know the group's attitudes (what they find acceptable, what they reject, and what they have no particular commitment to) could this help you tailor your approach and get better results? How can we measure attitude? Communication Scientists have asked similar questions. Their research has confirmed that discovering what is important to our audiences, and knowing their attitudes about topics, is a crucial factor in determining our effectiveness as message senders.

Carolyn and Muzafer Sherif, authors of *Social Judgement Theory*, have done extensive research involving the evaluating of attitudes (Social Psychology, 471-492). Social Judgment, "The judgment of attitudes" (Littlejohn, 126), underscores the usefulness of measuring attitudes on any given topic. As the message sender attempts to introduce information and to persuade, the degree to which a person accepts, rejects, or is uncommitted to a topic is important. The clearer the sender's understanding of the receiver's attitudes about the topic, the more tailored the message can be to reach desired results. (Sherif. Social Interaction, 330)

In this paper, I will cover the concepts and processes of Social Judgement Theory. I will identify the theory in scientific terms. I will evaluate the strengths and weaknesses of the theory. I will illustrate the theory's usefulness. I will show how the theory can be applied using a communication episode.

The subject of attitude judgment and its role in communication processes is of immediate and practical use. Some of the more obvious benefactors of Social Judgment Theory are commercial advertisers, politicians, communication strategists, lobbyists, and lawyers. Teachers and consultants also assess audience attitudes regularly and use what they learn to design certain messaging.

Social Judgement Theory has proven to be beneficial to many different kinds of communicators. The theory has been utilized since its formal introduction in the mid 1960s. My work on the following pages explains and demonstrates the theory. The work serves as evidence that the theory is consistently useful as we progress through the 21st century; an age where communication is the focus of the global community.

History and Theory Development

On September 13, 1965, Muzafer and Carolyn Sherif introduced Social Judgment Theory in a paper titled *Social Judgment-Involvement Approach to Attitude and Attitude Change*, during a meeting of the American Psychological Association, in Chicago. The Sherif's theory set out to accomplish a valid model that could be used to more accurately measure social attitudes. They felt that Osgood's Semantic Differential technique, which measured attitude using bi-polar adjectives (i.e., good vs. bad) on a 7-line evaluation scale, was not adequate. The Sherifs write,

> "The social judgement-involvement approach assesses the extent of acceptance and rejection on significant social issues without imposing mixed measurement indicators that represent the individual's stand on an issue as a single point (for example, as a mean or a single composite score). ...The present approach continues in the tradition of social perception or social judgment." (Social Interaction, Process and Products. 342)

Where Osgood's model showed only one response to a topic, and that being either positive or negative, the Sherifs' model showed degrees of acceptance or rejection of a topic. For the purposes of persuasion, for example, Sherif wanted to show the relevance of audience latitude of acceptance, rejection or noncommitment to topics. Sherif saw the importance of considering these measurements as a speaker attempts to persuade his/her audience to accept a position other than the one they find most acceptable. I will demonstrate this theory later in the paper using a case sample.

To develop Social Judgment Theory, Muzafer and Carolyn Sherif used, "as an important basis of their approach to attitude and attitude change, principles developed by experimentalists (Social Interaction. Selected Essays by Muzafer Sherif). They referenced works by Carl Hovland (Psychological Methods), Beebe-Center (Affective Judgment, 1932), John Volkmann (External and Internal Anchors Relative to the Object of Judgment, 1964).

Concepts (Major Variables)

The concepts or major variables of Social Judgment Theory are: *a) The Latitude of Acceptance* which is the range of statements on an issue one finds acceptable, *b) The Latitude of Rejection* which is the range of statements on an issue one finds unacceptable, *c) The Latitude of Noncommitment* which is the range of statements on which one is not committed, *d) Ego Involvement* which is the degree of personal relevance an issue has (Littlejohn, Theories of Human Communication, 126. Sherif, Social Interaction, 330.) and *e) The Discrepancy Issue* which is the distance between the most acceptable position of the receiver and the position expressed by the speaker. (Sherif, Social Interaction, 342)

Processes

Social judgment, the judgment of attitudes, is made by comparing a message with an internal attitude anchor. (Littlejohn, 126). Sherif designed an attitude measurement scale featuring the following measurements (Semantic Differentials):

MA=Most Acceptable *A*=Acceptable *NC*=Noncommitment

R=Rejection

A person's attitude about a topic can be measured by asking their feelings regarding the acceptability of a topic, using a 7-line scale, as diagrammed here:

Extremely Good	Moderately	Slightly	Neutral	Slightly	Moderately	Extremely Bad

The person's first response is the "*MA*" response (Most Acceptable). The researcher will inquire at each line on the scale until the acceptable, rejection, and noncommitment responses are determined. From these findings we can measure a receiver's latitude of acceptance, rejection and noncommitment.

For purposes of influencing attitude change, the researcher considers ego involvement of the receiver:

"The greater one's ego involvement in the issue, the smaller the latitude of noncommitment, the greater the latitude of rejection, and the less the potential attitude change. Messages lying in the latitude of rejection do not facilitate positive change. Within the latitude of acceptance and noncommitment, the greater the difference between the position of the statement and the person's own attitude, the greater the predicted attitude change" (Sherif, M., Social Psychology, 491-492.)

For purposes of predicting communication behavior, "susceptibility to change can be predicted by the present approach from the size of the latitude of noncommitment as well as the size of the latitude of rejection." (Sherif. Social Interaction, 350.) Through their experiments the Sherifs' provided considerable evidence that support their theory. Researchers can use the attitude measurement scale to accurately *predict* communication behavior among audiences. This can be useful as speakers plan persuasive messages.

Further, "The position of a statement on an attitude scale is often distorted. The *Contrast Effect* occurs when one judges a statement to be farther from one's own position than it actually is." (Littlejohn, 126.) For example, if a highly ego involved person perceives that a speaker does not fully agree with *every* point of his position, or, if the speaker remains neutral on the topic, the highly ego involved listener will judge the speaker's message to be completely unacceptable. "The *Assimilation Effect* occurs when one judges a statement to be closer to one's own position than it actually is." (Littlejohn, 126.) For example, if a noncommitted or "slightly ego involved" listener perceives a speaker to be physically attractive or nice, that listener will be inclined to interpret the speaker's position as closer to their own even if the speaker's views on a topic are not exactly the same as the listener's views. "Statements that lie in one's latitude of rejection tend to be contrasted, while those in the latitude of acceptance are assimilated. Distortion by assimilation or contrast is accentuated by ego involvement." (Littlejohn, 126. Sherif, M. Social Interaction, 346-347.)

Identification of Genre/Perspective

Social Judgment Theory is a cognitive-behavioral perspective. The term "cognitive" refers to how we use our minds (cognition) to process information. The term "behavioral" refers to our action or response (Littlejohn, 126). The perspective is from World View II, where it is believed that people exercise "free will" and choice in communication situations. The individual mind receives, makes sense of, and evaluates messages within the scope of free will. The process of evaluating and judging messages involves choice. Sherif writes,

> "Being cognitive-motivational and behavioral systems, attitudes include more or less lasting assumptions about the world, premises and regular expectations about the way the world operates and people within it, beliefs and perspectives about one's own kind and other people, and sentiments and convictions about what is right and wrong and to be desired and to be

scorned...Some of [our] attitudes define what [we] exclude...The behavior from which an attitude is inferred always involves a comparison, a choice or a decision among alternatives. That is why the psychology of judgment is relevant to attitudes and their change...Changes in categorizations may be taken as indicators of attitude change..." (Sherif, C. Social Psychology, 471-472.)

World View I Scientists focus on cause-effect, ruling out choice and free will as options in communication situations. World View II Scientists (Sherif) believe that people exercise free will as they select and execute communication behaviors. There are no pre-set laws that dictate human communication behavior according to Social Judgment Theory.

Evaluation

In evaluating the theory, I will answer the question "How might Social Judgment Theory be extended, expanded or otherwise improved?" I will evaluate Social Judgment Theory by looking at scope, heuristic value, validity, parsimony, appropriateness and openness. (Littlejohn, 38-39)

Social Judgement Theory covers a broad domain. It can be applied to many people in many communication situations. Because it measures *attitudes*, it is not highly restricted to a specific group.

The theory has been useful in generating research and ideas. Muzafer and Carolyn Sharif expanded the research of Osgood, and others, and additional research has been done to test and expand the Sherifs' findings. More than 1,000 researchers have used or referenced the Sherifs' theories as we begin the year 2020.

There is data to support the theory. Attitude scales and related testing have been used many years since the 1960s. Consistency in reliability of results has proven useful to communication scientists, particularly in experiments to influence and predict attitude change. The theory has practical utility. It can be applied in a broad number of communication situations involving attitude about topics. Social Judgment Theory's attitude scale, for example, is uncomplicated and simple to duplicate. The major variables are few in number.

How Might This Theory Be Extended, Expanded or Improved?

Sherif does not address, to any notable degree, the problem of using only one attitude scale test per person to accurately portray a person's "true" attitude. If a researcher performs the attitude measurement test on a person who has a headache, is tired, or is distracted by other priorities at test time, will the researcher get a "true" or accurate attitude read? Environment and other influences should be considered as potential factors that can contaminate attitude readings. I propose that researchers consider such things as a person's social maturity and age, also. For example, would a young person (more inclined to try to please or gain approval from the researcher, i.e., a pre-teen) be more prone to tailor his/her answers, compared to an older more socially mature person who is likely to be more set in his/her ways and not intimidated by the research process (i.e., a senior citizen)?

Sherif's methods give us a general idea of a person's attitude range, but not necessarily an accurate measurement. The researcher should perform several tests per person, at different times, to determine the continuity of the subject's responses. We can improve Sherif's theory by performing multiple, identical, attitude scale tests on each person, to ascertain a more accurate measurement.

The Practical Implications

The practical implications for Social Judgment Theory are that we can use this theory to construct messages for particular audiences, and increase the likelihood that the audience will accept, or be open to the message. If we learn the attitudes of the listeners, (their feelings on a topic by range), we can know the most effective ways to introduce information, and when needed, to persuade. The theory's attitude measurement scale is very useful in creating message approaches to appeal to the audience's preferences and bias. For purposes of persuasion, this is particularly beneficial.

Conclusion

Using Social Judgment Theory can help speakers know how to approach sensitive or controversial issues, and what to emphasize to win audiences' confidence. When speakers want to persuade listeners, the theory helps with message construction for that purpose. The theory's attitude measurement scale can help speakers prepare and deliver messages that are in line with audience inclinations to listen. It helps speakers predict and understand receiver behavior.

It is not enough to have a message and an audience. Speakers should know the best way to articulate their messages so that they will be received. Social Judgment Theory provides the tools to help speakers reach their audiences effectively.

References

Littlejohn, S. (1996) <u>Theories of Human Communication</u>. Belmont, CA: Wadsworth Publishing Company

Sherif, C., Sherif, M. (1969) <u>Social Psychology</u>. New York, NY: Harper & Row Publishers

Sherif M. (1967) <u>Social Interaction: Process and Products</u>. Chicago, IL: Aldine Publishing Company

Notes

Practical/Career Applications of Communication Theory

The Culture Industry

Analysis of Adorno and Horkeimer's *Theory of The Production of Culture*
By Elaine Patricia Walker

Culture can be boxed, shipped, advertised and sold. It comes in a dizzying variety of shapes and colors. It is generally labeled "high" or "low." High culture and low culture are packaged separately but in today's economy, both are often excessively priced. Culture is big business.

When German theorists Adorno and Horkeimer came up with the theory that culture is actually produced by industry, they were primarily motivated by a fear that people would forget the horrors of the Holocaust. They drew a connection between the manufacturing of culture and desensitization. They warned that culture was being manufactured for the purpose of controlling or at least manipulating reality. As the masses begin to rely on the images and sounds of manufactured culture, the masses become detached from what their true reality is. For example, the past and the present as seen through the lens of manufactured culture, is a watered down, neatly packaged version of what really happens. Looking at copyrighted versions of the past, (i.e., books featuring the Holocaust) would replace feeling and remembering in a more personal sense.

Adorno and Horkeimer said that culture doesn't just happen; "Culture is a result of powerful forces and intention." Powerful people create, package and sell culture. The production process is the foundation of the culture industry.

Although these advocates from the Frankfurt School of Thought offered arguments within the context of a post-war climate, their "culture as a product" theme is more apparent today than when they wrote it. Film, television, radio, computer and print ads are the means by which culture is produced and introduced to the masses. Using these vehicles for communication, culture can be more efficiently manufactured and explained even as it changes to suit the economic goals of the powers that be.

One of the key words in this concept is "production" (production as in assembled, promoted and sold for the purpose of consumption). Consumption is another key word. The production of culture and the consumption of cultural products provides the foundation for this "culture industry". Adorno and Horkeimer wrote that culture is "consumed uncritically" by the consumer. Consumers give over the production process to industry and rather passively accept whatever is presented. It is this passivity that is at the heart of the theorists' concern. I gather from their argument that they were most concerned with the consumers' lack of resistance and their silence when being force-fed. Could this non-critical, non-thinking attitude be encouraged? Adorno and Horkeimer warned that it most certainly could be. When someone else fashions your reality and assigns levels of value to it, they own your reality. If they can sell it to you, they own you. One's self-perception of reality can be determined, to a great extent, by the culture industry.

There are three properties of culture mentioned in the readings. The first is repetition. Here, the theorists explain that the goal of culture is to impress the same stamp on everything. For example, I write one message (book, post, blog, tweet, etc.) but I duplicate it many times to distribute it. Culture is shaped by the selling of the same product (and messaging) over and over again. The second property is that culture is uniform and whole. Culture might wear a business suit in one instance but a basketball uniform in the next. Whether it's packaged in a tight dress and high heels or a nun's habit, the culture product is interchangeable. Culture can cross-dress and hold simultaneous positions in the media (RuPaul, Dennis Rodman, Madonna.) Consumers learn to take in culture however it is presented. Culture is digestible whether served online, by radio, film or television. The third property is that culture begins to control politics and art. Mass media and mass culture are part of one whole. Violence is a part of the whole also. Violence is an open, raw power that operates within culture. All of these things; politics, art, media and violence are interconnected with culture. Power is what moves it all. When powerful people demonstrate their power, they seem to become even more powerful. As power grows, culture stops being an artistic notion, and becomes strictly business. The business becomes the practice of using power. People accept the growth of power even when the power is used against them. This is why the powerless sometimes respect their oppressors; they become infatuated with power as a good thing even if they never have direct access to it themselves. Hitler's rise may have been a result of this phenomenon. Hence, Adorno and Horkeimer's warning.

Earlier, I mentioned the key terms production and consumption. Distribution is another key term. Adorno and Horkeimer explain that culture encourages consumption. If something is wanted by the masses, a lot of it has to be produced. Culture allows few points of production but many points of distribution. For example, a movie producer makes one version of one movie, but has it duplicated thousands of times and shown simultaneously all over the nation. Today's internet facilitates the culture industry through mass distribution.

Distribution causes a reliance on technology. In the movie example above, I explained the duplication/distribution process. This massive distribution is made possible by technology. Technology plays a significant

117

role in the culture industry. Access to technology is class based. The more money you have, the greater your ability to use and even influence technology. The upper class, then, have the advantages afforded by technology. Some of the advantages are that technology is the fastest way to convey information. He who designs the information and the messages might not own the means by which it is relayed. Consumers utilize technology, but they don't necessarily control how technology is used.

The more advanced the technology the more powerful the upper class. Technology also closes the gap between work and social life for the lower classes. For example, an employee driving to his/her job once had the luxury of enjoying an uninterrupted ride in to work. Now, a boss can reach him/her by cellular phone anytime! There is less and less personal time available to the average worker. The upper class are certainly in a position to benefit the most from technology.

I have selected two magazine ads that illustrate the culture industry at work. The ad reads *0% FAT*, but it refers to an automobile. The car appears to be suspended on a popsicle stick. In modern culture, weight consciousness is a big deal. Nonfat foods are featured in ads and on store shelves almost everywhere you look. Since visual ads are so plentiful, readers tend to glance at them without reading them. This car ad cleverly uses a food image to capture the eye of the modern reader. The car is purple (a noticeable, bright color) and it is brightly lit in the center of the page. The 0% FAT line would appeal to a modern reader of a woman's magazine or digital ad. After you notice the ice cream bar is really a car, you read the faint colored text. The first line is "Here's a cool treat that you won't feel guilty about." This would only make sense during a period when so many consumers are weight conscious.

The other ad uses terminology unique to the present day. It reads "Surf the Interstate," borrowed from the phrase "Surf the internet" (computer jargon for browse through data on a broad computer network system). The ad does not sell computers; instead, it sells Dodge cars. This kind of ad could only work in a computer-based society whose culture includes sophisticated technology.

Culture is created, distributed and understood with the aid of technology. The ads I selected are samples that tell us what is important these days (0 fat and computer literacy). Ads also highlight what is valued in culture. Through the culture industry, the masses get a sense of what is important, what is acceptable and what gets rewarded. These things change however, so the masses are constantly hungry for what is the most "in" at the moment. Technology is the feeding tube. The culture industry provides the "food." Bon Appétit!

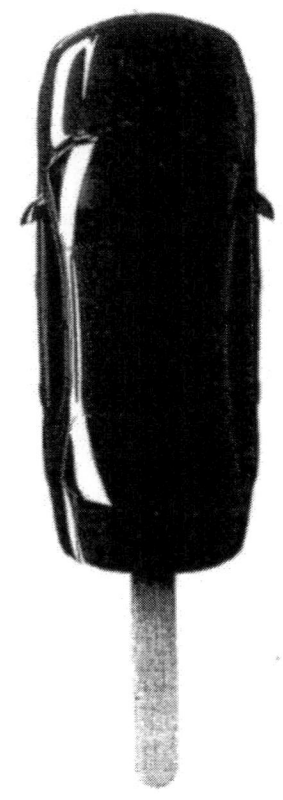

0% Fat. 100% Fun.

Plymouth Breeze $15,330* (Nicely equipped.) Here's a cool treat you won't feel guilty about—Plymouth Breeze. No extra calories, just plenty of room. And it's filled with features you crave, including standard air. To get a taste of Breeze, see your Plymouth dealer, call 1-800-PLYMOUTH or visit the Web at www.plymouthcars.com

One clever idea after another. That's Plymouth.

*MSRP includes destination, excludes tax. Brush after every meal. Floss regularly.

Surf the Interstate.

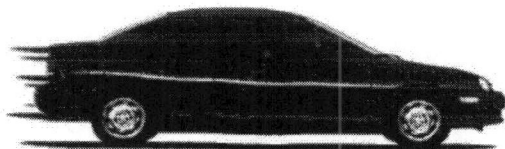

Hi.

Here's some information you can really use on the superhighway. The cab-forward Dodge Neon has a surprising amount of room for you, your friends, and their stuff, to boot. There's an available sound system with eight speakers in six locations (very important). And because its zoomy, 132-horsepower, multi-valve engine is linked to a fully independent suspension, Neon is anything but a hard drive.

For more information call 1-800-4-A-DODGE or surf on over to our Web site at http://www.4adodge.com

Neon Coupe & Sedan 🐏 The New Dodge

Under $10,400 for starters.   Around $13,300 nicely equipped.

Your MSRP after $500 cash back, includes destination charges, but excludes tax.

Always wear your seat belt.

Retelling Stories

ROBIN HOOD MURDERED BY A NUN

England- Robin Hood, leader of The Outcasts (banished citizens of Nottingham living in Sherwood Forrest) and two companions died after eating soup laced with Nightshade poison, early afternoon, November 2, during a stop at a convent forty miles south of Sherwood Forrest.

The Abbess of Kirkleigh, living as a nun since the deaths of her brother, The Sheriff of Nottingham and her long-time lover Sir Guy of Gisbourne, prepared soup laced with poison and served it to Robin Hood, John Little and Friar Tuck when the men visited the convent seeking first-air during their travels toward Sherwood Forrest. One year prior, Robin and his followers rescued the King of Nottingham, King Richard the Lionheart, who had been captured as a prisoner of war and held three years in a dungeon in Austria for ransom. Upon King Richard's return to his throne in Nottingham, he restored citizenship to all Outcasts, gave Robin and his wife Marion a place of distinction in government, and executed the Sheriff and Sir Guy of Gisbourne for crimes of tyranny. The Abbess of Kirkleigh, who for many years during King Richard's frequent absences, joined the Sheriff and Sir Guy in acts of violence against the citizens, escaped execution and hid out in a remote area, living anonymously as a nun, secretly plotting revenge against the King and Robin Hood.

The Abbess confessed to the murders, telling Much, the miller's son (a friend of Robin Hood) that she laced the soup with nightshade poison to kill Robin and his men, whom she held responsible, in part for her brother's and lover's deaths. Much hanged the Abbess after she confessed to the murders, then he returned to Sherwood Forrest where Robin's widow, Marion, and their young son Martin, had relocated.

Robin Hood was heralded throughout England as a defender of the poor. He was labeled "an Outlaw" by the Sheriff of Nottingham during the absence of King Richard because Robin spoke against the Sheriff's mistreatment of the poor. As a young child, Robin watched his mother die of starvation after the Sheriff and his men burned down his family's crops, burned other food provisions and killed their livestock, because Robins' family did not have enough money to pay the Sheriff's new high taxes. Robin and his grieving father became penniless survivors.

Robin's father Martin was an excellent archer, who killed free-roaming deer and gave the meat to the hungry poor. The Sheriff claimed that all deer belonged to him in the King's absence. One day, the Sheriff caught Martin during a deer hunt, dragged him into Nottingham, and with Sir Guy of Gisbourne, cut out Martin's eyes and sentenced him to death by hanging in the city square. During this time, the distraught Robin was befriended by Marion, one of the Outcasts, who lived in Sherwood Forrest. Robin was taken in by the Outcasts and soon decided to try to rescue his father, which he did successfully. Upon Martin's safe return to Sherwood Forrest, he taught the Outcasts to use the bow and arrow.

Later, a monk named Ignatius fled the tyranny of the Sheriff and joined the Outcasts. They gave the monk a nickname. "Friar Tuck". He was an expert swordsman. He taught the Outcasts to fight using the sword.

Much, the son of the town's Miller, was the best wrestler in England. Much's father was burned alive by the Sheriff because he could not pay more taxes. Much became an Outcast and taught them all to wrestle. Robin became leader of the Outcasts, and they grew in number from 100 to approximately 500, all skilled fighters an all victims of the Sheriff and Sir Guy.

Sherwood Forrest was en route to Nottingham, so many travelers passed through. The Outcasts robbed only the rich travelers, using that loot to care for the poor. It was the Sheriff's plan to get rid of the poor, handicapped, and albinos. Robin's efforts to care for them enraged the Sheriff. Robin's wife, Marion, and his son Martin were both albino.

For years, Robin and The Outcasts successfully defended themselves against the attacks of the Sheriff. Robin Hood escaped the sword, the arrow, the noose, and hundreds of trained soldiers seeking to kill him. It is of great note that Robin; England's greatest archer Tuck; a noted swordsman, and John; a skilled fighter, were all murdered by a woman of small stature, a nun, armed only with a bowl of soup.

Extra Credit:

Find the Loyola Marymount University clue.

<u>Answer:</u>

Who is Ignatius?

Values and the Globally Connected University

By Elaine Patricia Walker, Ed.D.

How do we define "a good education"? Should a professor, a student, a university, be concerned with what is good? Values were an important topic of discussion in the early universities. I encourage the discussion today, more than a decade into the 21st century.

From the first attempts to form universities in ancient Greece, to the establishment of well- known institutions such as Oxford and Cambridge in the 16th century, the notion of a complete education included the teaching of values. The university's focus on values persisted even as the early church insisted that, outside of the home, the church, exclusively, should teach values. In *The Idea of a University* (1898) by John Henry Cardinal Newman, we read an argument for a liberal education. Newman stated that the goal of a liberal education is to make people "better". The pursuit of excellence, particularly excellence of mind, produced the "better" and was thus an important element of a complete education. Newman added that a good education produces good citizens. The writer interpreted the idea of "good" as that which promotes excellence of character and that which fosters community. Newman suggested that the teaching of morality cannot be separated from a good education.

Today's universities are connected through technologies that enable us to learn and share in many different ways. Students are able to participate in lectures via satellite. The image of a professor or expert who lectures at a university in California can be beamed live to Japan and her voice simultaneously translated from English to Japanese. A student in a classroom in New York City is able to speak with and complete an experiment with a student on a sea expedition in Russia, via remote telecast. How should professors address morality and values from culture to culture? How will we discuss values in the globally connected university?

As the university extends its global reach, it is important to deeply discuss what is universally and consistently good. How we treat our neighbors, how we share information and resources, depends on how we *value* others. The university is the ideal place to think through the new dynamics of globally connected "classrooms". The university is no longer limited to a physical place. As educators use computer-based environments to enhance teaching and learning, we must consider values as we prepare students to live and serve in our globally connected world.

Without attention to morality and values, it is possible for a university to continue to conduct research, share information, reimagine our existence, and grant degrees. But *why* we should do all of this will be lost. We will have a variety of machines and technology that help us to connect, to process and share information, to preserve ideas, but without moral grounding, will our activity support a common good? Can the university offer a good education without a focus on *the good*? Today, more than ever, the university is not merely buildings and reputation. The university is human beings, bound together by mission, learning together and working across time zones and across oceans, hopefully, for some shared good. How do we approach the concept of the good in today's university? Do values still matter? Whose values do we honor? What is the meaning of "a good university education" today?

What it all Means

Lecture on Interdisciplinary Inquiry and the Question of Meaning

By Elaine Patricia Walker, Ed.D.

Life in a human body – what does it all mean? Can humans ever understand our origin, and what a creator meant to accomplish when He (She, They?) made a universe and a world? Earth and billions of galaxies? Why?

What is the meaning of evil, suffering, the death of the innocent, especially children? Why is violence so prevalent in nature and among humans? Animals kill and eat other animals. Insects eat other insects. Humans destroy other humans, and some are self-destructive.

If we live in a world where "only the strong survive," what does that kind of world mean for those "strong enough" to live there, and for those who are devalued as "not strong enough"?

Shared Meaning

"Meaning" is complex. My attempt to investigate meaning is subsequently complicated. Can meaning be deconstructed as a knowable, shared reality?

Such as it is, shared meaning is a foundation for consensus, which is needed for humans in community. How humans arrive at shared meaning is an almost miraculous occurrence. I am intrigued how we, as the many, are guided by one truth. "General Consensus" can be assumed active when people just go along with the more convincing voice as an act of survival. That is not how I describe my notion of "shared meaning." I refer instead to the agreement that is genuine, mutually acceptable, and driven by reason and evidence. Meaning that is mindful of the other, and all in the community. It is through this position that I explore "what it all means."

Personal Meaning

Everything means something to someone. Meaning is deeply personal. A hug could mean something beautiful to one person, but a hug could also hold meaning that causes pain. For example, a hug can be a precious gesture of love for the happy newlyweds, or it could be a horrible prelude to torture for the sexually abused child.

We have learned that humans can have what appears to be the same experience, but that experience holds very different meanings for different people. Meaning then, is personal, based on individual memories and one's processing of experiences. The past is experienced only once, in a collection of moments remembered, but it influences our "now" and sometimes it impacts how we will process our unpromised future.

The Human Brain and Meaning

Everything that our brains encounter is filtered for meaning. We search for meaning as we interpret words and silence, actions and inaction, and nuances in an environment. Meaning drives our decisions and intentions.

How does the human brain process meaning? Electrical impulses are activated and interacting constantly, even when we are asleep. Is meaning possible apart from the electrical activity of the human brain? Please refer to studies of the human brain. There are thousands of publications on the anatomy of the brain, brain function, and new discoveries of brain and mind. Neuroscience offers amazing facts and insights. We can also consider the fields of Psychology, Psychiatry, and Sociology as we discuss "meaning" and how humans process meaning.

An Intellectual Pursuit

For this lecture series, Philosophy, Psychology, and Sociology can provide a particular kind of guidance as we think through the complexities of meaning and human interaction with the concept.

It is the intense search for meaning that separates humans from other animals and life forms. For example, amoeba, starfish, fleas, birds, and moose do not use scientific methods or philosophical reason to search for the meaning of life. A complex intellectual pursuit drives humans in ways not found among other life forms. Perhaps contemplating meaning is unique to humanness. That humans are deeply curious, prone to record their findings, and determined to discover the meaning of life, leads me to conclude that we were designed to inquire.

Most life forms simply live. They do not question "why" they live. Most life forms are focused on survival, their next meal, satisfying a nature-driven desire for mating, and sleep. Humans are preoccupied similarly, but humans also pursue pleasure with greater commitment, and we often ponder the unknown. For those humans who seek control or power, this obsession is usually for self-satisfaction, an off shoot of pleasure, or an appeasement of fear. The study of human behavior, and thus human thinking, can be enriched as we join our strengths across disciplines. Discovering what it all means is a journey.

The Interdisciplinary Approach

The journey is the thing. The search itself is the thing. Finding meaning can be explored in different ways. Through the lens of different areas of study, and certainly different methodologies of inquiry and testing, we can examine meaning from several angles. I highly recommend an interdisciplinary effort to search for meaning.

I gather that all branches of science, all disciplines of study, can contribute to our understanding. We might only reach a deep understanding of "meaning" when and if we share our search for it. Our areas of expertise, our specialties, might come fully alive when we compare and collaborate. Perhaps, meaning (the full story) might only be achieved when we put our discoveries together like a puzzle. We might not be able to understand completely, unless we realize that at our best, within our own disciplines, we only have part of the answer. It will require all disciplines to contribute and to be respected for their contributions.

It appears that we humans are driven "to know," to seek, to wonder why. What three questions do we want to explore? Let's dissect the questions using an interdisciplinary approach. I look forward to your proposals.

Poetry and Lyrics

Be Him

Rescue me from the shallowness
of lesser men

Be Him
Find me

I wait, I grow, I build,
I trust God, for you

For you. Find me!
Be Him

Written by Elaine Walker

Double X

I am Double X
You are X and Y

Get to know me better
I'm already inside

That X chromosome
In your DNA
Binds us together
In a special way

It's genetic, by design
It's the science,
And it's divine

Double X
Deal with it
You are you and me
Deal with it

Double X
XX, XY

Double X!

Written by Elaine Walker

Gifts From The Fire

Look where love brought us
What love should have taught us,
we never learned

We took what love gave us
Love should have saved us
What we built, we burned

Now we're on our knees
Searching through the ashes
Looking for what's left of what's gone

Where are the gifts from the fire?

Lyrics by Elaine Patricia Walker

Hatred

What does hatred want?
Can it be satisfied?
Will hatred stop itself after all its victims die?

Does hatred ever sleep?
What is hatred's goal?
What does hatred reap?
How does it seep into a soul?

What is hatred made of?
How does hatred thrive?
Do you weaken it with love?
Have you helped it stay alive?

Who do you hate?
Why do you hate?
How does hatred serve you
since Hate hates you too?!!!

By Elaine Patricia Walker

I Got Away

He broke one too many things
My heart, then my wings

I couldn't stay
But I couldn't fly
Got away

Didn't want to die
I chose life
Even though he broke mine
He broke mine

But I'll be fine
I'll be fine
Because I got away

Written by Elaine Walker

Irreverence

This pain has no compassion
It refuses to kill me

It wants to be entertained, when I should be sleeping
When I pray, it laughs irreverently

As I hurt beyond description
even now
it wants to dance

Written by Elaine Patricia Walker

Nights Since September

(Honoring the grieving from the attacks on the USA: NYC Twin Towers, The Pentagon in Virginia and Flight 93 that crashed in Pittsburg.)

These long nights are not natural
They have forgotten how to end
They obscure the remains of attacked things
They cover the invisible graves that are the unwanted reminders of this new war

Nights since September
they linger
Perhaps to cloak the suddenly dead;
Those thousands not fully found but definitely there

A peculiar darkness
Years later, we remember what has never left us
The grief finds its place and is understood here
In the long night made eternal through historic recollection
Nights since 9/11/2001
persist
They have forgotten how to end

Written by Elaine Patricia Walker

She Entertains

She sparkles
And you like that
She wears the dress you like
It's made of invisible knives
She dances in the spotlight
Shines so bright
Sharp and dangerous

Your lust pushes you close to her
And you get cut,
But you don't back up
Because you like it

You ignore your injuries
You bleed all over me
Your life ends at her feet
You are slashed and slayed,
Broke and played…

Entertained…..to death.
Oh, how she entertains

Elaine

Take This Pain

A heart broken into pieces
Finds its way onto the page
Starts beating for the world,
On display, at center stage

A private pain that slayed me
(as I kept it to myself)
became a melody that saved me
may it save somebody else!

Take this pain
It will dance with you
It offers music too
It rhymes, take this pain

My pain writes the songs
Lyrics right the wrongs
Helps us manage what we feel
Makes us dance, helps us heal

Take this pain....

Written by Elaine Patricia Walker 2015

The Traffic in Us

We write
so that others can step inside of us, to see themselves
in all of our human glory and shame
We let the world in

We sacrifice our right to "normal"
We sacrifice sleep and privacy
so that we may bleed for others

We admit what we see in our flawed reflections
We work hard to become mirrors: a difficult preoccupation for human
flesh

We invite all to the read
We endure the traffic in us
to give others the chance to live
lives less interrupted than our own

Written by Elaine Patricia Walker

When to Learn the Lesson

Are the lessons on the floor?
Learn them there, or
Learn them on the ground.
You can't learn in the grave
Learn when to learn the lesson

Lessons -
Learn them as a witness
Or learn them as a victim

'Can't come back from the dead
Learn the lesson while you live
and breathe –
It's too late when all that you can do
is die or grieve

Learn
When to learn the lesson

Lyrics by Elaine Patricia Walker

Sermons

Disbelief

By Elaine Walker

The act of disbelief requires an object for denial. When I say that I do not believe in something or someone, there must be something there to deny. I refer to *something* when I say "not that" or "that is not real" or I do not believe in that. The "that" is real, if only for the purpose of saying it is not.

Denial can be a coping reaction. When a person expects some desired end but experiences less than the anticipated good, the mind must decide how to process the disappointment. The emotional self makes adjustments to survive future uncertainties. These adjustments help people to function beyond their disappointment. One attempt to survive the disappointment is to deny its importance. This is common in cases where people looked to someone, or some power, to rescue them or to help someone they care about. A request was made for intervention and use of power on their behalf. The powerful source did not respond as anticipated, so you deny that they are powerful, or deny that they exist at all.

The denial of a reality, a truth, or a being does not change the existence of the thing. When someone says there is no God, for example, their denial can suggest that the God they deny is the God they once appealed to for something that was not given or granted or changed. If a person feels abandoned by God, in most cases, they do not want to feel that pain. Denial is one way of addressing pain. It does not work over the long-term as ignoring emotional pain causes physical malady and exacerbates psychological trauma.

If God did not exist, people would never have appealed to Him. People would not be hurt that God did not help them as requested, when requested, and exactly how requested, unless they believed He is real. People would not spend even a second denying that God exists if they did not expect that He does exist and that He was there listening to them when they called on Him. God would never enter human consciousness if He was "not". Some people have said, "God if you are real, then do this for me…". Clearly the asker believes that God exists. Who are they directing their request to? To ask of someone, I have to believe that the giver is able to meet my request. I ask because something in me knows the giver is real, and able, and there.

I could have no expectation unless I have faith. Faith in this case is simply a belief in something or someone that I cannot see, but I know exists. I have to ask myself, "Do I exist only when I can be observed or understood?". The answer is "No". I exist even when people cannot see me. If I am in one city, and you are in another, you cannot see me, but that does not mean I do not exist. If you speak French and I speak English, we both exist regardless of our ability to understand each other perfectly. If I have not yet met someone you know, like your father, you know that your father exists regardless of my never having met him. You know your father and can attest to his realness, his existence. I have a relationship with God, and I can attest to his realness, even when He does not do what I ask.

Many people have a relationship with God, and there are many ways to describe God. The variation in description of God has caused some people to think that there is no one true God. I am known by my family as one name, by my coworkers as another (Dr. Walker), and by my friends as yet another (a nickname). My grandchildren call me a name that no one else calls me. Only my daughter calls me Mom. I am one and the same person.

I do not change. People's perception of me changes depending on our relationship. I am daughter only to my mother, so she has a unique way of referring to me. I am known differently among the different groups of people that comprise my frequented circles of interaction, and I might be described differently by them. At work, I might wear a suit or a research jacket, while around my family they see me in casual attire. I wear different clothes to church, and so on. All these different expressions of myself, but I am always me. God is known by people in very personal ways also.

If your biological father abandoned you, you might say "I don't have a father". The truth is you do have a father. He simply was not around. If you feel as if God abandoned you in any way, you might say, "There is no God". But there is a God. God wants to talk with you, heal you, empower you in this human life. The Bible scriptures, especially the preached Word of God, can reveal to you the plan for a life of balance, spiritual health, and deep abiding joy found most fully in a relationship with God. Try again. Call out again. Believe. He's listening.

Scriptures:

Luke 24:25	John 20:3	Psalm 27:13	Acts 11:21
John 3:16	Romans 3:22	Psalm 116:10	Ephesians 1:13
John 11:40	2 Corinthians 4:13	Matthew 8:13	
John 17:20	Hebrews 11:16	Matthew 21:32	

Gravity Bends Light

by Dr. Elaine Patricia Walker

I live on a planet that is "strategically suspended in space" (Sagan. Pale Blue Dot). Who arranged for this? Who designed all of the energy and the matter that defines this world? Who invented the gravity that governs movement? Who created all of the light that makes my life manageable? I could not appear on the earth and live as I live now without giving thought to these questions.

I know that I did not create myself. I did not create the earth, the air, or other people. But here we are. As far back as the human mind can determine, to that first moment of creation, a power greater than the created product was already there. That power created "there". That power was not you, not me.

Someone made you and put you here. Why? Where did you come from originally? Where were you when your unique fingerprint and genetic identity were designed? Who decided that you would get the opportunity to come to earth as a human? Who decided that the first human should exist? Who created the conditions for perpetual human existence?

Through my questions, I make an admitted attempt to explore the origin of pure power, the origin of the beginning, and the "why" of human existence. In my limited human capacity, I am yet inspired to probe the complexities of origin and human purpose. Like others before me who have broached this controversial topic, I expect a variety of reactions to what I offer here. I wonder aloud, and I encourage your thinking and reflection.

I understand that humans have discovered amazing truths: personal, scientific, and spiritual. However, all of the research and discoveries that humans have compiled pale in comparison to the source of all knowable things. For every person that has figured something out, do ask how this was possible. Who made you able to use your created brain in the ways you can use it? Who provided the subject matter for you to study?

I posit that someone supplied original matter for all that humans can observe or measure. Someone generated realities that are the precursors to human thought. Someone placed Earth where it is, among all the vastness of the universe, and decided that life should exist here. Someone sustains life here. Someone started it all. Scientists, theologians, philosophers, historians, artists and thinkers contemplate the origin and "being" questions. I join that discourse.

Scientists look for evidence that can be known. "The statements of science are not of what is true and what is not true, but statements of what is known to different degrees of certainty" (Richard Feynman, Physicist). Theologians respect evidence as they seek truth that is revealed by God. Revelation stands outside of the limits of human deduction, but it is not contrary to it.

Consider this truth: Someone created this world and determined, without your permission, that you should be here. You are one of billions of people on a planet that you did not create. You came into this world as a baby, completely vulnerable upon entry. You remain vulnerable throughout your time on this earth. Nature, human behavior, and any number of other factors can be destructive or unpredictable. Regardless of the attempts at control, humans cannot completely control the world. This may be an unsettling fact, but it is true.

Someone smarter than you designed a universe and placed you in it. I acknowledge this creator and I call this creator God. Those who deny God's existence do so with a mouth and a mind that they did not create.

Throughout this discourse I will refer to God as "He". I do so with the understanding that God transcends gender. How writers refer to God can lead to heated debate. This writing will not address political, social, or theological arguments in that regard. My focus is God and the created human being, in relation to a few of the more dominant forces that impact human existence on planet earth and our surrounding universe. I pay special attention to gravity and light in the human experience.

God's creations interact with gravity and light in extraordinary ways. Investigating the relationship between light, gravity and the human experience on earth is my way of honoring some of the great questions that have stirred thinking people for centuries. I hold the position that God's creations are marvelous, numerous, and originally wonderful. It is apparent to me that the creator had and has only the best intentions, regardless of the human influence on his product, and human interpretations concerning them.

Humans these days get about 25,550 mornings in a typical life span. I pause to appreciate my mornings. A logical place for me to begin is to study the light that makes each morning possible.

I have early and sustained ties to light. My parents named me Elaine. The meaning of the name Elaine is "Shining light". I was born in the state of California, known for its sunny weather. My nickname is Sunshine (some call me Sunny). I have always been intrigued by light. Its physical properties and its figurative reach are fascinating.

In this discussion, I consider light from a scientific perspective and from other perspectives. There are several different approaches to the study of light. As we explore, let us consider light in the many ways it has been investigated throughout human history. Since light is essential and eternal it deserves considerable attention. Many people have investigated light, over time. I hope that you will personally examine all of my claims and my findings.

There are a variety of ways to explore. Philosophy is occupied with the search for truth. Theology seeks to understand the nature of God through examination of religion. The sciences investigate matter and behavior. The arts interpret notions of life and living. All of these methods have merit. Each discipline offers illumination. I am inclined to look through every available lens.

Scientists say that humans are celebrating our ability to investigate with more precision, to theorize with more confidence. However, scientific and philosophical pursuits offer only pieces of insight into our complex and magnificent existence. I offer my work with these limitations in mind.

While it is reasonable that I should investigate my existence, I realize that I am more than my body and its experiences. Intellect has its place in human investigation. As a researcher, I respect what can be replicated and verified.

I also seek to know beyond the limits of human intellect. I seek to know the original source for everything. In this, I seek to know God. I must note here that when a human seeks to know God, human intellect is not enough. Intellect is a good tool supplied by God. I claim here that God is the source of intelligence and knowing. However, God operates above human intellect. God is Spirit and God is revealed on a spiritual level. Intellect can help humans to think about what exists, but to understand existence itself and the author of existence, the spirit of the human must be engaged.

Man can study what God made (by man I refer to the human species). Man can describe and interpret things of this world, and man can try to explain phenomena. Man can invent useful things, clone life, destroy life, and claim to be a god. But man is mortal. Made, dependent on a creator. Man is not, nor will he ever be, GOD. This GOD is the ultimate creator, the origin, the truth.

Before truth is discovered or supported by humans, it exists. Truth does not rely on scientific methods or human reason for validation. Science has not figured out why humans exist, why the universe exists. There are reasons and answers, but the truth of our existence eludes scientific discovery.

The late Stephen Hawking said that the ultimate triumph of human reason is to find the answer to why it is that the universe and we exist, "for then we would know the mind of God". To know the mind of God is an intoxicating pursuit. We cannot know the mind of God using human reason alone.

I am not certain that the human brain can manage the complexity of knowing God fully. The brain is physical, housed in flesh, constructed to do specific tasks. God created the brain and the human who uses it. God is not subject to the thoughts of people. God is Spirit and superior to humans. Our mortal attempts at understanding God, using only our brains, may be futile.

Humans are prone to believe in only what we think we can prove or what we need to believe for survival. Understanding God, the creator, will require insights that derive from spiritual places. Nevertheless, for the sake of starting the exploration, I think we can start with something we all experience. Let's look at light.

Light has the mysterious property of being both a particle and a wave. Scientists accept that light can be fully one thing and fully another at the same time. Before the scientific documentation of this fact, the duality of light existed.

In the bible, Jesus is described as "the light of the world..." (John 8:12) and God is strongly associated with light. Jesus is identified as simultaneously fully human and fully divine. In scripture, Jesus referred to his dual nature as he explained his identity ("The father and I are one..."). Jesus' revelations about light and twofold existence were not presented in his time on earth in the same way that scientists publish it today, but the premise is identical. Jesus spoke of this truth then scientists confirmed it thousands of years later. It was true before Jesus said it. It was true when the people around Jesus did not understand him as he said it. Man's ignorance concerning light did not change the truth about undiscovered light. Man's ignorance about Jesus does not change who Jesus is. Although work in our new science proved the duality of light, this truth existed before science clarified what Jesus said.

Albert Einstein is credited with the discovery that energy and matter are two different forms of the same entity, that matter can be made from energy, and that the flow of time is not a constant. In his famous equation, $E=Mc^2$, the E represents Energy, m is Mass (the material stuff of the universe), and c (celeritas-the Latin word for swiftness) is the speed of light. This energy is an invisible presence at the core of all matter. Original energy is not restricted by time. Who enables this to be true?

All matter is first invisible energy regardless of its final form. Energy is required to produce everything that becomes visible. Energy in its purest form is light.

In the book of Romans, chapter 1, verse 20, Paul writes "... the invisible things of him from the creation of the world are clearly seen, being understood by the things that are made...". What humans can see is a byproduct of what was first invisible, often in the form of an idea. (The Bible)

Consider a chair. The first chair existed initially as an idea. Later, the chair was built. When the chair was an idea, it existed, albeit in an invisible dimension. The unseen is another state of being; the origin of the "real". An idea is energy. Energy precedes matter. Matter, or the visible, is energy in a different form. This truth might help us to understand that we existed originally as an idea in the mind of our creator.

The account in the bible of the creation of the first man includes a creator physically designing a man, then bringing the man to life. The male of the human species carries both the X and the Y chromosome. The female carries only the X chromosome (two of them). All humans begin with the X chromosome. The introduction of the Y chromosome determines if the sex of the human will change from female to male before birth. The genetic material in the first man was used to form the first woman. This makes scientific sense, but it was true before science could confirm it. People of faith simply accept the truth before scientists learn enough to agree with God.

Faith has no need to measure for proof. The light that man can measure is not the only light there is. For example, there is the immeasurable light of God's love. There is also the light that is accessible for human calculation. The speed of light is roughly 186,282 miles per second, the fastest known velocity in our universe. Light travels at a rate of 1.3 seconds from earth to the moon. It takes sunlight an average of 8 minutes and 20 seconds to travel from the Sun to the earth. Earth is about 92.96 million miles away from the sun. Cosmic history is determined in light years. Still, there are forms of light that remain scientific mysteries.

Recent experiments suggest that the gases found just beyond the earth's atmosphere accelerate light movement. Light behaves differently as we move away from the earth. Our universe bends around the speed of light so it appears that nothing near earth can move faster than the speed of light. However, billions of light years away from the earth the facts may display differently. There is certainly more to know.

This we do know: Gravity bends light. Isn't that interesting? It is interesting that it is true and interesting that humans would discover such a truth. Einstein's research on gravity began in 1905 and was finalized in 1915. He spent roughly ten years working on his hypothesis. On May 29, 1919, during a solar eclipse, Sir Arthur Eddington experimentally measured the bending of light and soon confirmed Einstein's predictions. As light moves toward earth, the gravity created between the earth's moon and the earth causes light headed toward earth to bend. Some force greater than gravity has set into motion a splendid order in which anything that comes near earth must contend with light and our gravity. This was true before Einstein, or any other human, discovered it.

In time, someone might find a reason to expand on or further explore theories of gravity and light. As humans, we discover new information as we stay open to truth wherever we find it. Truth is no person's sole property. Truth must be shared. What we know about light does not make light a truth. Light is, regardless of how much we know about it at any point in time.

Optics is the branch of physics that involves the study of light. In this area of science people who are interested in optics study how light is produced, how it is transmitted, how it is measured, how it is detected and how it is used. They study the visible light spectrum, which is the rainbow of light that we can see from red to violet, and ultraviolet and infrared light.

Scientific studies show that light travels slower through water, through glass, and through human eye lenses. Light bends when it goes through glass. Light travels in waves, which are also called electromagnetic waves. Light waves can reflect, refract (change the course of energy), and be absorbed. Light reflects when it bounces back off an object. When light waves reflect, they bounce back from the surface at the same angle that they hit the surface.

Gravity slows down light. To be more precise, a gravitational field slows light. A typical delay is some hundreds of microseconds. Stronger gravitational fields cause a more severe warping of time. Brian Greene, author of The Elegant Universe (2003) said "... Breathing life into space and time by allowing them to curve, warp and ripple, results in what we commonly refer to as gravity".

Einstein concluded that light can exist only when a light wave is actively moving forward. This fact supports the claim that nothing on earth moves faster than the speed of light. What about forces that are not confined to the earth? What about light that exists beyond the earth's boundaries? What rules govern a universe that humans cannot fully measure?

Symmetry and Order: Evidence of a Creator

The universe is big. In comparison, I do not take up a lot of space. I grew from an infant to an adult, changing in size over time. I am now approximately 5 feet 3 inches tall. The length across my shoulders is about 18 inches, the same length if I measure my feet placed toe to heel. My body has symmetry, and my skeleton is ordered. I was designed. The length from my elbow to my middle finger (18 inches) matches the total length of my outer thigh and the length from my knee to the heel of my foot. The span of my chest area from underarm to underarm is also the same length across as the toe to heel measurement. From the base of my neck to the area beneath my navel, there is that measurement again: 18 inches. My body did not fall into place through random coincidence.

From my beginning, before I was allowed to develop in a human womb, I existed. I was someone's idea. I was a consideration. How did I grow into their design? It is an incredible journey from invisible energy to becoming a functioning being on a known earth! There was an order to my history.

First, I was designed, then a fertilized egg, then a developing person inside a mother's body, then born, then breathing on my own, then growing on an earth governed by gravity and light. So too you had a beginning somewhere. You were designed on purpose.

So much of who we are as humans exceeds the observable. We are our thoughts as much as we are our actions. My thoughts precede my actions. My voice, my written words, my behaviors; these are symbolic of my thoughts as my thoughts remain invisible. My thoughts are real although you cannot see them. When you see me in any format, in person, or my image through a broadcast of some sort, you see my body. My active body in the process of sharing my thoughts is a representation of who I am. My invisible thought-life is the seat of my existence. When you see things and people in the world around you, you are a witness to the manifested invisible. What can be seen was first imagined. Take that line of reasoning as far back as possible and you will get to original design. Go further back, and you will find the original creator.

Science may not be able to fully explain origin if it ignores the God who created human origin. To investigate anything, the scientist uses a created brain and materials that are already provided by that God. One argument in this regard centers on who created what or if there is a "who". Man did not create God. There must be an original "who". Spirit precedes flesh. As scientists like Einstein attested: Energy precedes matter.

Scientific inquiry is one way to study phenomena and matter. The scientist proposes that something is or is not, or that it might be. Then a hypothesis is tested, results are recorded, shared, and replicated. Scientists examine manifestations. What comes before the manifestation? Who caused it to be there for the scientist to discover? Is "it" less real or less possible before it is discovered? What fuels scientific imagination and theories?

Scientific methods are ideal for certain types of measurement or investigation. Scientific research is a means to provide evidence and to verify that which already is or that which is likely to be. Science is a tool for understanding. Science is not truth. Science helps us to find truth. The best practices in the sciences are conducted with absolute honesty. Too often scientific practices are corrupted by human ego.

Human ego gets in the way of pure discovery. Human progress has been hindered by the unchecked desire to be praised, to be considered a god, to be perceived as right or first, to "be powerful", to the detriment of truth and accuracy. As we continue to search for answers, we must create safe places to ask questions. Abuses of the ego prevent this.

I read somewhere that the human ego is often at odds with the eternal order of things; it is out of step with the divine. To acknowledge the divine, humans must admit that we were created. Since we were created, someone existed before we did. This someone was not, is not, another human. This someone created humans.

Many humans respond more favorably to that which can be seen and manipulated by human intervention. Since humans cannot see God, control or measure God, their creator, some find it easier to pretend that God does not exist. Some humans, hurt by or disappointed about an experience or outcome, blame God or hate God. Blame and hate require an object for those emotions, so in these cases the person actually believes in God. People question a God who allows tragedy and human suffering. If pain is present, then, they suppose, God is not.

Some humans deny that a god exists beyond the god they have made of themselves. In matters of human flesh and the ego that serves it, there must be a god. There must be an object of praise and power. If the ego refuses to praise the ultimate creator, then it will seek the praise that rightfully belongs to God. Many people want to be perceived as powerful or they desire to be near power. Why are praise and power so important to humans?

Who is the designer that orchestrated human desires and needs? It is the same power who created light and gravity and the material for everything you can know. Just as humans design and manufacture products, providing a guide for best use, God has designed humans and God provided a guide for us. That guide, that "best way to be human", is found in Jesus, the light of the world.

Many people do not know Jesus. Many people do not know the laws of physics. It is possible to live a life on earth without knowing either. My life, however, has been enriched by learning about both.

I see how science and faith work together. Science explains God's creations and resulting marvels. Faith believes in the God who makes science possible. The scientist provides evidence for that which faith already knows exists. Faith comes before science. The unseen origin of what is, always precedes the visible.

The laws of the universe existed before humans discovered them. The laws were in place before humans could understand them. The laws function even if humans do not believe they are operating and even if humans do not explain them accurately. God exists and He created the basis for the laws, regardless of human unbelief or denial. Ignorance of law does not nullify it.

The standard model of particle physics says that invisible particles called quarks exist. No one can see quarks, but scientists insist that they are there. The scientist operates in faith. Something unseen exists. Humans do not see God as they can see each other. I was created by this God who has made it possible for me to know that I exist. I am able to feel the life in me. I do not feel quarks or most of the invisible but undeniable properties of the universe. Why would the scientist who admits that invisible quarks are real, not admit that the God who made the quarks is more real? Is something real only if you can see it or understand it? Before it can be seen, discovered, or fully understood, it must exist.

The reported resurrection of Jesus is not the only time that the laws of physics were altered on Earth. Healings, miracles, and wonders done by Jesus, and witnessed by many during his life on Earth, defy the traditional laws of physics. Since God made man and his environment, God can operate above the laws that govern his creations.

The laws are put in place for routine stability. Sometimes, I think that God likes to shake things up.

Operating above the physical laws is the supernatural. I have heard it said that God is the "Super" and man is the "natural". It is possible for God to fully manifest in, and through, a human body. Jesus is the best example of that. The creator of human bodies made a body for himself, put his living word in that body, and went through the process of the human experience. Why?

The bible explains that God loves the humans he made although humans were, and still are, terribly disobedient and unbelieving. It is pure love that necessitated that God save the creations he made from their own destruction. So God came in the earth personally, legally, sending his word in a body, to walk in human time and ransom humans. Jesus accomplished this beautifully and completely. God as creator could stay on His heavenly throne, while his word lived on the earth. Brilliant! God's Word existed in the beginning, and His Word created humans and their world. The visible word of God is Jesus:

> "In the beginning was the Word and the Word was with God, and the Word was God. He was with God in the beginning. Through Him all things were made. In Him was life and that life was the light of men". (John 1:1-4)

Light was part of the birth of Jesus, and the absence of light was part of his temporary death. A brilliant shining star marked the location where Jesus was born, serving as a guide for those who were sent to welcome Jesus to the earth. Read the birth narratives in the bible for details. In the book of Matthew, Chapter 27, Verse 45 records the following about the moment that Jesus died on the cross: "From noon onward, darkness came over the whole land until three in the afternoon". There is the theme of light again.

Most descriptions of God include light, a bright light. The humans that God made were originally clothed in light. As an animal's hair grows from inside, eventually covering the animal to give it a protective coat, the glory of God was inside of humans, and it shined from the inside out. The glory was the original cover for humans. The light was extinguished after humans disobeyed God. God's glory cannot shine through disobedience. This is when the first humans realized that they were naked, with only skin as a covering. Skin is subject to the elements of the earth, to decay. Without the glory as protection, everything changed about how humans would live on the earth.

Evil cannot abide in the presence of God's glory. Holiness cannot tolerate evil. Humans need another kind of access to God's glory since it no longer inherently resides in them. Adam and Eve lost the light within them, but in time, Jesus came, full of God's glory and light, to redeem that which was lost.

Jesus is not a religion. Jesus is living light that came to the earth in the form of a man, to live in complete obedience while in a human body, restoring the original plan of God. God gave to humans a free will to make their own decisions. This free will ensured that a decision to obey God was voluntary and was therefore pure to God. Humans, sadly, decided to disobey God. The consequences are great as sin and pure light cannot coexist.

Sin, once exercised, is relentless. A sin committed will not rest or die on its own. Sin is insatiable. Sin lives in and thrives in the dark. God knew from the beginning that if humans chose to disobey, this would usher in unspeakable darkness for humans. The darkness is a spiritual darkness that is quite profound. The type of darkness humans allowed in through disobedience refuses any part of God. Separation from God results in utter darkness of the soul. The soul that rejects God languishes in the dark where sin is in charge. Sin punishes its followers. God is the ultimate and original light, but God is more than the opposite of darkness. While darkness is characterized by the absence of light, light exists always, even when darkness cannot. Light is a constant. When we trace matter to its origin, we find light at the core. Light is our beginning and our destiny.

Light is stronger than darkness. Light cancels out darkness. A person must decide to accept the light. Some people are so lost, so deep in the dark, and have been in that condition for such a long time that they do not know that they can be rescued. Every human soul that God made is eligible for rescue through the love of God. Some people have experienced such pain and disappointment that they struggle to love, or they do not know how to believe in love.

God's love is different from human love. God's love illuminates all life. The closer you get to God, the brighter the light force within. Darkness has to leave. Peace of mind, forgiveness, the ability to rest, joy, and a desire to live -all these good gifts are found in the light.

Humans can begin to learn of God's love as they study and believe Jesus. This is where life begins, in the light, in Jesus. As you continue to learn about Jesus, you will learn what God expects of humans and what great love God has for us.

What humans believe about Jesus is important. Jesus said that the most important truths to live by are to love God with all your heart, mind, soul and strength, and to love your neighbor as yourself. Love then is the key to managing this existence and thriving in this life. Loving God and loving your neighbor as you love yourself can be a great challenge for some people. Some people do not love themselves yet, so it is impossible for them to truly love others. Some people love only themselves, so they seek their own pleasure at the expense of others. Some people have been disillusioned or hurt by experiences that were supposed to be all about love. Some people have been terribly wounded by others in this life. Some people are going through the motions of living, but they are so lonely, even though they may be in relationships or surrounded by crowds. Believing in true, lasting, pure love has been difficult for some. Good news: Healthy love is possible and available, and it is wonderful.

God has an exquisite love for you. The best way for humans to begin to experience God's love is by first acknowledging God. Start with a private conversation. Just tell God your truth. If words escape you, God understands even your groans and the language of your tears. God will listen to your heart. God made your heart, so He understands it best. A powerful transformation begins when you talk to God from your heart, and when you listen to Jesus.

The act of talking to God suggests that you believe He is there. Talking to God is a demonstration of faith. Faith is necessary for this relationship. Just as someone would have to acknowledge that you exist to develop a relationship with you, you must acknowledge that God exists before you can develop a relationship with God. A close relationship with God will positively transform your life. God knows that you exist because He made you. God is gracious and kind so He will not force himself into the forefront of your life. I encourage you to invite God in.

Details vary about God, how people get to know God, and how people worship God. I do not propose a particular religion to you in this writing. God is concerned about relationship. He already knows you, and He wants you to get to know Him. I ask that you look at your life and think about how you got here. Your conversation with God might begin with questions for Him. Ask.

If God who made you does not exist, how can you exist? How can you explain the amazing order in this world? Look at mathematics for wonderful patterns that suggest higher-level order, often beyond our complete comprehension. The sciences help humans to see magnificent order; order that existed before humans discovered it. Through God's grace and generosity, humans are allowed to discover, using brains and realities that God created.

God's wisdom is infinite. So many scientists do acknowledge the splendor and amazing properties of the earth and the universe beyond. Unfortunately, too many scientists acknowledge their own forms of wisdom, but they have not yet given honor to God who has made all of their wisdom, their discoveries, their triumphs, possible. Some scientists do acknowledge God. To those scientists who do not yet honor God, I reach out to you in respect and ask that you take a closer look at your denial. Why don't you believe?

Some scientists have said to me that they do not believe in the God of Jewish religions, nor the God described by Catholics or worshipped by Protestants, or the God of Islam or Eastern religions or tribal gods or anyone else's God. I ask, "What about the God that made you?" If you are intelligent, where did that capability come from? Do you really exist? If you exist, why would your predecessor not exist?

There is no proof that God does not exist. In fact, millions of people know that God does indeed exist. Just because you may not have entered into a personal relationship with God, does not mean that God is not real. If I never met you, I could claim that you do not exist. I may have heard of you, your family would insist that you are real, but because I have never met you personally, I could continue to claim that you are real only because your family and friends think that you are real. Or I could say, "I do not know you yet". In the case for God, millions of people across thousands of years testify with their very lives that God is real. They got to know Him. They began by saying, "Jesus, come into my heart now. Show me who God is."

God is waiting for you with love like you've never known before. You can be delivered from the gravity of this life; the things that weigh you down or pull you toward harmful thoughts and actions. Gravity bends light, but it cannot break it or dissolve it. Strong forces may have knocked you down, or kept you down, but God has new life for you, in His light.

Maybe your life seems whole as it is. Perhaps you feel balanced and fine without God at the forefront of your life. One need not accept God for the primary goal of feeling happy. It is not my objective to solely promote the fringe benefits of a life centered in God, although truly the benefits are many. Life on earth is temporary, but your spirit (the real you) is eternal. The author of your eternal nature wants the best for you. You will not experience God's absolute best for you while you manage life on Earth in a perishing human body. God is Spirit. The best is reserved for your spirit being. You are spirit first and finally. It is your spirit that gives you identity as a living being. Your body simply is the temporary house for your spirit while you live on Earth. What about after your body dies? Where will your spirit live? What is the connection between your earth life, and eternity?

You were created by God and placed on this earth for a reason. Since God made you, it is logical to assume that this God has a reason for doing so.

Your purpose for being on this earth, in this human form, is revealed in God. God wants you to realize fully the purpose for your life. God wants for your spirit to live, in the best circumstances possible.

I believe that you matter. Every person created by God has a divine and important purpose. I hope that you believe this, and that you find good answers. I caution here that your personal beliefs or my personal beliefs do not make something factual. Humans do not devise truth. The creation and establishment of truth is the responsibility of God. When God's truth is discovered, it should be shared to uplift humankind. I believe that Jesus is God's truth, presented in a way that humans can understand it. Thoroughly investigate Jesus, for yourself, and see what you find.

God already knows all that we will eventually discover. Let's be mindful of God in our learning and expression. Scientists, artists, thinkers; this is my special invitation to you as we continue to seek, ponder, and discover!

References

Albert Einstein, Physicist. Theory of Relativity. Inspirational quote: "If you can't explain it simply, you don't understand it well enough".

Richard Feynman, Physicist, Author of The Meaning of It All (1998).

Brian Greene, Physicist, Mathematician, String Theorist, Author of The Elegant Universe (2003).

Inspirational quote: "The boldness of asking deep questions may require unforeseen flexibility if we are to accept the answers".

Stephen Hawking, Mathematician, Professor, Author of A Brief History of Time. (1988).

Carl Sagan, Astronomer, Astrophysicist, Astrobiologist, Professor, Author. The Origin of Life on Earth lectures.

The Bible, Thomas Nelson, Inc. Publisher (2015).

Gravity Bends Light: Questions from the Text

By Dr. Elaine Patricia Walker

Page 1, first paragraph

"I live on a planet that is strategically suspended in space. Who arranged for this?"

"Who invented the gravity that governs movement and place?"

"Who created all the light that makes this life manageable?"

Page 1, third paragraph

"Someone made you and put you here. Why?"

"Where did you come from originally?"

"Where were you when your unique fingerprint and genetic identity were designed?"

"Who decided that you would get the opportunity to come to earth as a human?"

"Who decided that the first human should exist?"

Who created the conditions for perpetual human existence?"

Page 2, first paragraph

"Who made you able to use your created brain in the ways you can use it?"

"Who provided the subject matter for you to study?"

Page 7, second paragraph

Albert Einstein…original energy is not restricted by time. "Who enables this to be true?"

Page 10, fourth paragraph

"What about forces that are not confined to the earth?"
"What about light that exists beyond the earth's boundaries?"
"What rules govern a universe that humans cannot measure?"

Page 11, second paragraph

"How did I grow into their design?"

Page 12, third paragraph

"What comes before the manifestation?"
"Who caused it to be there for the scientist to discover?"
"Is 'it' less real or less possible before it is discovered?"
"What fuels scientific imagination and theories?"

Page 14, first paragraph, last sentence

"Why are praise and power so important to humans?"

Page 14, second paragraph

"Who is the designer that orchestrated human desires and needs?"

Page 15, first paragraph

"Why would the scientist who admits that invisible quarks are real, not admit that the God who made the quarks is more real?"

"Is something real only if you can see it or understand it?"

Page 20, fourth paragraph

"Why don't you believe?"

Page 21, first paragraph

"What about the God that made you?"

"…If you are intelligent, where did that capability come from?"

"Do you really exist?"

"If you exist, why would your predecessor not exist?"

Page 22, first paragraph

"What about after your body dies? Where will your spirit live?"

"What is the connection between your earth life, and eternity?"

Hunger

by Elaine Walker

Animals are driven by hunger. Think of wildlife. One animal eats another. Predators hunt their prey on land, in water, in the air. Humans also kill other animals, and other living things, to eat them. Hunger drives all animals, all insects, all fish and fowl, all living creatures with a digestive system. Hunger drives humans: the animal at the top of the food chain.

Any undisciplined hunger, not submitted to God, hurts and ultimately destroys the human body. It seems that most animals live to eat, and eat again. The hunt for food is an ever-recurring activity for many species. Eco systems are managed, to some degree, by animal predators that control over-population by their eating and hunting patterns. Humans operate on a different scale. Thoughtful control of appetite is necessary to prevent over consumption. Overeating results in physical health problems and diminished quality of life.

Hunger is an intense force. The more intense the hunger, the less compassionate the hungry being. The hunger drive is devoid of compassion. Compassion restrains a being from doing harm as a meal is sought. If humans are not conscious of the power of the hunger drive, behaviors to satisfy appetite can compel a being to take a life to sustain its own.

Undisciplined eating can be dangerous. Humans often eat too much of what we find pleasurable. The unchecked hunger drive insists that the pleasure we experience through taste be repeated again and again. Some food and drink items that humans consume are addictive. Chemicals in sweets, salty foods, high fat foods, and even some meats, can be highly addictive. Too much of anything can be detrimental to good health. God cautions humans to practice modesty, self-control, restraint, and to seek balance. Jesus spoke often of subduing the flesh. The spirit and mind of a person takes precedence over the body.

Hunger is a natural response, but it is not always rational. A hungry person eats and is satisfied. The body extracts nutrients from the meal and eliminates the toxins and most of the material food product. The less healthy the food or drink, the more likely that the body will not benefit from what is consumed. When fat from food is stored, this causes the liver to be less productive and puts stress on the body's systems. A cycle of diminished organ health occurs over time. Hunger that dictated the impulse to satisfy a biological urge, when unmonitored, can feed ferociously, wildly. This can lead to gluttony, a sin because it destroys a body that God made.

The body *can* be trained to eat and drink a reasonable, healthy portion and learn to be satisfied. Serving sizes should be ample enough to feed one person, not three. Often the size of the drink and meal is too large for one person. Even if the portion is served too large, we can consume less in one sitting.

Many Christians will not use illegal drugs or alcohol. Many have been delivered from vices that are not compatible with godly living. But overeating is a central activity of many church goers. Eating primarily for pleasure can become a vice. Pleasure seekers are insatiable. Food can become a drug, an addiction. Overeating or eating inappropriately is an area of access for the enemy of God's holy church. If people destroy their health with too much or the wrong kinds of food and drink, then we reduce our effectiveness and we compromise our witness.

Where to start to fix this problem? To begin to rewire your brain, replace sugary drinks with water (Sugar is highly addictive. The more you ingest, the more you want). Eat smaller portions (for each item on the plate, it should fit in the palm of your hand). Your body will make a gradual, natural adjustment. Eat healthier foods more often. Include steamed vegetables 4 times per week, fresh fruit no more than once each week for the first 40 days. Subtract one bad food each month, for one year. If you are already a sugar addict, my suggesting that you cut out cobbler, pies, cakes, cookies, donuts, candy, and sweet coffee drinks, might send you over the edge! Know that you are an addict if even the thought of no sweets makes you mad.

You cannot change food habits using your will alone. Food intake triggers chemical reactions in the body. Personal will power has its place, but God's will supersedes it all. Will God help you? Yes, He will.

Appetite covers only one dimension in the human experience, but it is expansive. Appetite is seldom satisfied for long. It seeks what it wants, gets it, only to be driven again and again to the same end. The same unfulfilled state, repeats. We struggle through the same process of desire, seeking, finding, consuming, and feeling temporary satisfaction. We devour foods and drinks that upset our stomachs, make us gain unwanted weight, or compromise our health. We do not want to abuse food and drink. But, we do, all for the taste of something, or the effect of pleasure. Something so powerful must be given to God.

Think of David, who became king of Israel. As king, he already had wives. Yes, plural, more than one. Still, he summonsed a married woman after secretly watching her take a private bath. He had his henchmen go and get her from her home. He had sex with her, got her pregnant, then had her husband killed in an attempt to cover up his sin. The woman's husband was a loyal soldier for King David. A desperate appetite causes destruction. If its focus is to please the body, it must be submitted to and governed by God's Word. Lust is lust. Lust produces unhealthy patterns because it never gets enough.

If human lust reigns, then the human is reduced to a mere animal, doomed to the inevitable destruction of a restless body in search of the next meal. God wants more for his crowning creation. Do not allow appetites to govern your existence. Instead, let God govern you. God is Spirit, so you will have to yield yourself at a spiritual level first. As your spirit follows God, your body will follow.

Enjoy food but do not let it rule over you. If you know more about the best places to get food, than you know about what Jesus said, then your priorities need an adjustment. Food is a gift. Food is necessary. Food is often an important aspect of expressing culture and caring. Food can be used for great good, and it is to be enjoyed. The bible is filled with examples of feasts and ceremonial uses for food. Jesus used food in holy activity. Think of communion. The devil certainly considered food, and tried to corrupt the good in eating. Adam and Eve, God's first "man" was tempted to eat something that God asked Adam not to eat or even touch. Why is food such a central part of the human experience? Why did the devil use food to cause man to disobey God? The devil has always tried to corrupt the good intentions that God has for food. God wants us to enjoy meals, cook for one another, share our food, and so forth. The enemy of God wants to taint that with gluttony and excess and misuse. Jesus is quoted in the bible as saying, "Take, eat, this is my body which is broken for you". He spoke these words as he sat at the table with his disciples, his friends. Jesus spoke in spiritual terms, not literal terms, in this instance. Jesus was speaking symbolically of the unity that he hoped to have with those who desired to be one with God, using bread for body and wine for blood.

Think of the popularity of films and television shows today, that feature vampires and evil beings that claim to literally drink human blood and eat human flesh. The devil tries to twist spiritual references to eating. God provided fruit and herbs for food, to original man that he made in His image. The devil used food to corrupt that precious gift and compromise man's relationship with God. Why did food work?

Think of the many shows and films that feature cooking and drinking alcohol and eating to excess. Restaurants are all the rage. Food magazines and food networks are everywhere! Why this obsession with food? Americans, in particular, are overweight at all ages. Why?

As humans, we must put food in its place. How do you begin to do this? Start by acknowledging God, in *His* place. God is first.

Uncontrolled, repetitive indulgence feeds the flesh and at the same time, destroys it. Be aware. Ask God to help you with your appetites. Remember, if the aim is to please the flesh, ask for God's help to control it, to guide that drive.

Think about the role that food plays in your life. If there is balance, then that is good. The devil wants us to be extreme. He will encourage bulimia and anorexia and starvation. Those behaviors/illnesses are not of God. Eat, and enjoy food the way God intended. No extremes.

In my experience, cooking for someone, and sharing a meal, is an act of love. Food is good. Misuse of food and drink is bad. Let's remember to address this God's way. Take back the power from the enemy of God. Remember that from the beginning, the devil used food to try to distance people from their God. Today, we take back the gift. We pledge to eat and to drink responsibly. We invite Jesus to dine with us. He wouldn't have it any other way.

The Power of Service

February 2016
By Elaine Patricia Walker

One of America's great writers and noted intellectuals, Ralph Waldo Emerson, was once an unhappy "P.K.", a Pastor's kid. He came from nine generations of pastors and ministers. He knew a little something about church life, from the inside. Among the many literary works he produced, he shared profound insights on the traditional Christian church and those who serve it. In one of his famous essays titled *Self Reliance*, he wrote: 'God will not have his work made manifest by cowards". I submit to you today that true servants of God must be brave. A church worker once said to me: "To serve church folk, you have to be crazy or anointed." Look at your neighbor and say, "Thank God for the anointing".

God has sanctified service as the highest calling in the human experience. In the book of Matthew, Chapter 20, Verse 28, Jesus said: "The son of Man did not come to be served, but to serve"… Jesus provides the best example of a servant.

Ephesians 6:7: Serve wholeheartedly, as if you were serving the Lord, not men.

Colossions 3:23-24: Whatever you do, work at it with all your heart, as working for the Lord, not for men. It is the Lord Christ you are serving.

Romans 12:11 reminds us that we must serve the Lord with spiritual fervor.

Philippians 2: 4-7 tells us to take the very nature of a servant, as Jesus did.

Reverend Martin Luther King, Jr. said:

> "Everyone has the power for greatness, not for fame, but greatness, because greatness is determined by service. Everybody can be great because anybody can serve. You only need a heart full of grace – a soul generated by love". Dr. King's words were inspired by the teachings of Jesus.

Greatness, in this life, is determined to a large extent by the service you render. Greatness through service makes an impact in spite of opposition or temptation. It is certainly not always easy to serve. For those of you who have never faced a time when you wanted to quit, when your work appeared to be underappreciated, your intentions misunderstood, your sacrifices taken for granted – if you have enjoyed a service environment free from trials – God bless you but that is NOT my testimony. But, "I still have joy. I still have joy. After all the things I've been through, I still have joy". Somebody who gets it, say Amen.

God's word encourages the servant and helps the servant to endure difficulties. In service, there will likely be difficulties. Haven't had any yet? Keep serving. Remember this scripture because, if you serve, you will need it one day:

> 2 Timothy 2:24: 'And the servant of the Lord must not strive, but be gentle unto all men"… "The Lord's servant must not quarrel, instead be kind, gentle to everyone, able to teach, not resentful".

If you can avoid it, do not argue, especially with those who are prone to discord. The person giving you an unmerited rough time has other issues. Pray for them. Allow God's word to speak to your heart, before you continue to speak to others during your service. What would Jesus say to the person who is contrary and difficult? Being a servant often requires great restraint and discipline. Servants are privy to inside information and private details of the served. Servants must be honorable and trustworthy. When people can't see the servant, God can always see the servant. Aim to make God happy as you serve. Honor God's word. "Thy word have I hid in my heart, that I might not sin against thee".

Sometimes, servants are placed in the most difficult circumstances. Onlookers might think that the servant is somehow less than the persons being served. They are not. Servants are often brilliant, discerning, wise, and talented. They are often very humble. Let me tell you a true story about a servant you may have heard about:

In August 1761, a little girl was kidnapped from Africa and shipped to America. She was estimated to be around 7 years old when she was purchased by the wife of a prosperous Boston tailor. Susannah Wheatley gave the child a name, as was the custom at that time. Phyllis Wheatley displayed exceptional intelligence. Within less than 3 years after her purchase ordeal, she mastered English, Astronomy, Geography, History, and she memorized much of the Bible scriptures. By her early teens, Phyllis became a "showpiece" in New England's intellectual circles. She was noted as one of the most brilliant conversationalists, white or black. By age 19, Phyllis was a published author. She corresponded with George Washington, Benjamin Franklin, and she visited with nobility during trips abroad. For a time, Phyllis became the best-known colonial poet in England.

With no admitted memories of Africa, Miss Wheatley eventually embraced a world that celebrated her brilliance but not her humanity. Her greatest dignity came from her service to Christ, not her obligation to serve her earthly masters. With all of her fame, she "belonged" to her female master.

She still was a slave, and an unpaid servant. She was purchased, never adopted by her white slave master. She made lots of money for her masters. Miss Phyllis Wheatley died in 1784 at a time when the color of her skin dictated her physical liberty. Though laws have changed, some attitudes have not. Even in the church, so many severely segregated on Sunday mornings. Sometimes service in the church and for the church demands that we pay attention to all of the realities of inequality, particularly those that might exist in the very churches we love.

Service to God is completely different from service to man. Nevertheless, the role of a servant is not easy. True servants are a minority. Servants are people of all ethnicities, but they form an often-uncelebrated minority. Reverend Dr. Martin King said: "The hope of the world is still in dedicated minorities. Trailblazers in human, academic, scientific and religious freedom have always been in the minority... It will take such a small, committed minority to work unrelentingly to win the uncommitted majority".

The power of service is evident in all great and lasting decisions for the good of mankind. This "good" is accomplished, so beautifully, through ministry.

Upholding and assisting God's leaders, is ministry. A servant might not get the recognition for a host of successes, but God sees all that is done. It is the servant who sustains the environments for progress to occur. A servant might not receive the respect from those served, respect that should be a natural response to selfless sacrifice and investment, but servants receive the reward of pleasing God.

The power of service is not felt in the process of "doing", but it is realized in the effects of a job well done. The power is manifested in souls saved, hearts encouraged, lives empowered for good. I celebrate this service that you give for the support of ministry. I acknowledge the power of service, a force that God has sanctified. Walk in that power.

Remember, your service is unto God. Holy service is for the purpose of bringing people to Jesus, the Christ. Jesus is the ultimate servant. The power of service is fully realized in spiritual salvation for the servant and the served alike.

Walk in the dignity of this holy choice. Service is a choice. Service is a path. Walk the path of service, and I guarantee that you will meet Jesus there.

-End-

"Y"

Male, Female and the Y Chromosome

By Dr. Elaine Patricia Walker

Genesis 1:26-27
26: "And God said, let us make man in our image, after our likeness: And let them have
 dominion…
27: "So God created man in his own image, in the image of God created He him; male
 and female created he them.

Genesis 2: 21-23
21: "And the Lord God caused a deep sleep to fall upon Adam, [anesthesia] and he slept:
 and he took one of his ribs, and closed up the flesh
22: "And the rib, which the Lord God had taken from man made he a woman
23: "And Adam said, This is now bone of my bones, and flesh of my flesh: she shall be called Woman, because she was taken out of Man.

From the creation account in the Bible, we read that Man was created first, then woman was created using material from the male. When this account was first recorded by Moses, he did not have the technology to study DNA, or chromosomes, or reproductive science. He wrote what God told him to write. Thousands of years later, we now have scientific evidence that proves the accuracy of the creation narrative in the Bible.

Believers accept the facts in the bible *before* scientific evidence echoes what God has already told us through his Word. Although faith has a longer history than science, both celebrate God's power and truths. Following is a bit of the science that supports God's creation of humans. This evidence answers the questions concerning *why* the male was created first. This is the story of "Y".

The "Y" chromosome is *one* of the two sex chromosomes in humans. The other is the X chromosome. The sex chromosomes form one of the 23 pairs of human chromosomes in each cell. These sex chromosomes, in particular, help to determine if a baby will be identified as a girl or a boy, male or female.

All babies at conception begin as female, with only the X chromosome contributed by the mother. The introduction of the Y chromosome causes an embryo to develop into a male. The man determines the sex of the child. Only the male can contribute the Y chromosome. Males carry *both* the X and the Y chromosome. Female "woman" carries only the X chromosome.

Male = XY Female = XX

Chromosomes are long pieces of DNA found in the center, the nucleus, of cells.

DNA is the material that holds genes. The SRY gene (sex-determining region Y) triggers development of male-specific body parts and via hormones, "maleness".

Chromosomes come in pairs. Normally each cell in the human body has 23 pairs of chromosomes (46 total in each cell). Half come from the mother, the other half from the father. The mother *always* contributes an X chromosome to the child. The father may contribute an X *or* a Y. The Y chromosome is passed exclusively from father to son. But when a son is conceived, that son has female DNA in him also (XY).

The male has female and male attributes in his cellular make-up. This is why the statement is accurate that "God made man; male and female". When God made man as male and imbedded both male and female chromosomes within him, God could then easily go within the male, and fashion a female out of the man. Thereafter, the reproductive process was set. Man is *male and female* at a cellular level. The word "man" carries an inclusive significance. The creation of the male first does not exclude the female or suggest that woman was less in any way. It was simply the prototype for human life.

Even God's references to himself as multidimensional, for example, "let *us* make man" makes sense in that God made man *in His own image*. A plural dimension is imbedded within God: God the father, God the Son and God the Holy Spirit. The plural dimension of "the male" man is therefore a logical outcome.

The female component of man was there at the beginning when man was created. The original word "Man" refers to both the female and male versions. *Hu*man means *person*. Although the male body was created first, female DNA was incorporated into that first body.

The early oral stories and eventually the written accounts of holy matters and human concerns, such as creation, were relayed by people who did not have the science that we have today. We can be certain that these ancient accounts were inspired by God. They spoke of things that were incredible and impossible to prove, at that time. Now, God allows humans to research his Word through scientific methods. We continue to discover more proof that God is who He says he is, and that Jesus the Christ is God's most reliable voice.

Science is not superior to imagination or to faith. Science is a means, a language through which we can investigate and interpret the world and the universe.

As a researcher I keep in mind that the methods of man are flawed. Man is a created being, attempting to study a world and a universe that we did not create. Some people claim that there is no God. It is that same God that gave them the mouth they use to deny Him.

The creation narrative is absolutely true as explained in the Christian Bible. It was true before science offered evidence of its validity. Researchers and scientists might eventually catch up with what we know by faith. Science does not *make* anything true. Science can only agree with truth. The bible states that God is truth and that Jesus is the way, *the truth*, and the life. I do not need science to convince me of this.

Science focuses on the observable, that which can be measured and replicated. Scientists investigate what God has already created using a created physical brain that would be nothing without life and intellect that God alone provides. Science is a gift from God to humans. Even science bows to God and honors His word. Science has proven the Genesis account.

Woman was essentially present when man was created. The female was inside the man.

Jesus explained that he is inside the Father and the Father is in him. "The Father and I are one" (John 10:30). Do we see a parallel here? God did truly make man in his own image!

Speeches

All Kinds of Wow

Welcome Address to the LMU Research Scholars Academy
June 22, 2016
Talking prompts by Dr. Elaine Walker

Welcome scholars! Wow!! You got in. (Recognition, applause)

Thanks to…

parents, families, friends, SMC partners, to all who support these students.
A supportive network makes a positive difference.

To the scholars:

1. Get ready for "all kinds of wow"!
2. Research can be exciting; filled with adventure and discovery.
    Serious wow (Cures). Amazing wow (Solutions)...
3. I welcome you to this program, and to the world of ideas.

Finding the Wow

1. Look for "wow" in the questions and interests of others
2. As you investigate claims and deconstruct arguments
3. When you contemplate, reflect, and notice

Giving "Wow"

Be you   Do the required work

Be a good listener   Show up on time

Try   Sleep

Celebrating the "Wow"

1. Getting in to this research academy, wow
2. Working with research mentors and university professionals
3. Growing as a person and as a scholar, wow
4. Delivering a research presentation on stage, wow
5. Celebrating the plan for your next academic milestone

Closing

Live a life of purpose, a life of "wow". Let your inner wow shine. We'll help you discover or create it. Here, at LMU, is a great place for creating "wow". All kinds. Scholars, let's do this!

An Uncrushable Joy for Learning

by Elaine Walker, Ed.D.

Today, I invite you into the world of fascinating ideas. In this space, it is safe to ponder different approaches to solutions. You are encouraged to imagine what could be. Concepts, lived experience, and new theories are heard and appreciated. Thinking is celebrated. Here, your voice matters. Here, we learn what is known, and we propose new ways of seeing. Learning is all kinds of fabulous, but it is also serious business. What sustains us as we learn? JOY sustains us.

Joy is a gift of learning. You will need that joy to anchor you in this program, and later in life. I hope that you discover an uncrushable joy for learning. How do you find it? That is the focus of my address to you this afternoon. The Undergraduate Research Scholars Program (URSA) is all about learning and growth, so it can be like a door that leads to a particular kind of joy. At URSA, we expect that each student is a thinker with an opinion. As scholars your opinion should be strengthened by facts. What you imagine can become tangible, or observable, or it can be otherwise experienced. How do you operationalize an idea? How do you clearly articulate and test a hypothesis? How do you examine facts and think through problems? How do you take a collection of thoughts and transform them into proofs or a solution? In this research program, URSA scholars will learn basic research techniques, and we will do work that encourages "learning how to learn". We have a fast-paced environment that can inspire you toward problem-solving and possibilities. Sound research helps to clarify a question, investigate phenomena, test claims and document the process of discovery. Today, you begin a special research intensive. This is exciting! Our world needs fresh, healthy perspectives. Our world needs you!

I began my research journey in 1977 at USC, as a new undergraduate student. My parents did not have the money to pay for my college education, so I had to put myself through college as an independent student. I do not have the time right now to share my whole university journey, but I can tell you that it was a struggle, largely due to lack of funds. Drama! I competed for and won scholarships, grants, and I had to take out loans. But, I discovered research programs along the way. Getting involved in research provided the momentum, focus and opportunity I needed to press forward from the B.A. to the Doctorate. No one in my family had ever gone to college, so I had to learn "all things college" on my own. URSA Scholars, you have academic mentors that will help you in this program. Reach out, ask questions. Be proactive. Use this time wisely.

There will be difficulties during your college experience. Do not give up! Push yourself to learn. Lean in. Try, and try again. Reach for joy in your learning experiences. Joy is there. You might find it inside of an idea. Open your mind. If you look for joy, you will find it. Look for joy as you examine something, or as someone asks an intriguing question, as you experiment, or whenever ideas are discussed. It might be a gradual discovery, but it is worth the wait. Once you discover the joy of learning, it will *change your life*. You will cherish it and speak of it often, as I speak of it now. Joy for learning is not something someone gives you. You cannot steal it or sell it. It is the gift of pondering, wonder, and discovery.

This uncrushable joy for learning propels us forward. It whispers. "Get up, find a cure, propose a solution, share what you learned, inspire innovation". "Fix something, build something, do something better. Help somebody". We all share this one planet. Research where we are, who we are, and what we can be. A joy for learning gives us strength and motivation for noble work.

The joy for learning grows with each new reading, each trek down an untried path. The joy keeps you company as you study. It animates your search and your findings. It will keep you energized and dedicated to the good. The more joy that you find in discovery and learning — the richer and deeper the joy. You might experience failed outcomes, disappointments, and lack of support. Deal with it. Because once you find that joy of learning – it is yours! It's uncrushable! The joy will replace a fear of failure. This joy will inspire you to seek answers and solutions instead of fame. Perhaps you will get a sense of this joy for learning in this research program. Stay open to it. Get ready for it!!

Welcome ELAC Scholars. I wish you God's blessings as you begin your journey in this summer research program at Loyola Marymount University. As you address issues in today's news, or lesser touted injustices, work with the goal of changing the headlines. Draw us toward rational solutions, peace, equity, mutually beneficial improvements, and progress that heals and sustains all of us.

Whether through spectacular learning adventures or quiet reflection, may you discover an uncrushable joy for learning. The Philosopher Rene Descartes said:

Je pense, donc je suis (in French) or

Cogito ergo sum (in Latin)

then finally translated to English:

"I think, therefore I am".

I say to you, "I learn therefore I have joy!" Scholars, learn and be joyful!!! Welcome!

-End-

Art Heals

By Elaine Patricia Walker

The last time that I was in this hospital conference room was the October 1st weekend of 2011, six short months ago. This place was the only room large enough to accommodate my family and our friends. We gathered here upon hearing the news that my 27-year-old cousin was in a horrible car crash that killed her 9-year-old daughter at the scene. My surviving cousin was brought here by helicopter to the LAC/USC Medical Center, with burns over 90 percent of her body. Her husband and her 4-year-old daughter, her mom and dad, her brother, grandmother, and many others who love her, waited and prayed. It was a long wait. Twenty days later, my cousin died. Here.

I will never forget the last time I was "here," or why I am here today. Being fully present, in this moment, in this place, is tender and powerful. There is a part of me that does not want to be "here" so close to such devastating memories. Please know that I would not risk the emotional and psychological investment unless I had something important to do with all of this pain.

This room I know. It was once filled with hysterics and whispers of the unimaginable, and crying, and love. Regularly used for Medical Education sessions and professional meetings, the hospital generously made this space available for a community of hurting people. My family and our friends will always be grateful for that kindness. While I certainly remember being here, I remember, far more so, the 5th floor.

I came to know *well* the Burn Unit on the 5th floor. I knew the sounds, the feel of the traffic of bodies and words. I knew the tense walls as I leaned against them in weaker moments. Art was the only distraction from the disfigured *everything* of those days. On the 5th floor as I exited the elevators, a special work of art greeted me. Mounted on a canvas the size of a door, were these vibrant flowers, painted in bright colors against a dark grey background. I paused to appreciate them. They always reminded me that there can be great and enduring beauty even among the ugly of scorched, wrecked, suffering. Flowers, so often thought of as fragile, perishable things, defied their reputation and they gave me strength.

I recall days when I discussed the artwork with my four-year-old cousin. One afternoon, as we stood near the painting, she told me that the flowers were happy. She pretended to pick one and gave it to me. I received the invisible flower from her and noticed that the artwork lost nothing, even when a child, with a healthy imagination, gently plucked from it. The flowers remained beautiful, still available for others to share. I took a closer look, a different look at those flowers. They *were* happy. I needed them to be happy, because on so many days, after so much bad news, I was not. I had to be strong for my family. I borrowed strength from the art.

Each time I visited the 5th Floor, I looked for and found the art on the walls. The art was always there. The art remained when the crowds grew thinner. It always brought a sense of comfort. The art healed my broken heart on one day and attended to my crushed will on another. The art conveyed necessary messages of hope and beauty even when the diagnosis changed, and the worst news came. The art was always beautiful. I could rest in it. It was my escape.

Austin Dobson once commented (in *Ars Victrix*):

"All passes. Art alone, enduring, stays with us.
The Bust outlasts the Throne..."

Art endures. Art heals. When medicine cannot, art heals. When words do not, art heals. Its presence in a hospital is vitally important. I work at a university that has an outstanding Art Therapy program in graduate studies. I know that research has shown the benefits of using art in therapy. But I know more perfectly, now personally, that art heals.

I take this opportunity to use my voice, my pain, my life – to encourage the placement of art in hospitals. This art will help so many people. Placing art in hospitals becomes a component of care, and it is the right thing to do. On behalf of all who are served here, all who visit, I express gratitude for the art.

Special thanks to the artist, Rachel Frances, for her work that continues to inspire and heal. Thanks to Barbara Oliver for her invitation to this meeting and for so many acts of kindness. 'To Martha and Toby for their gracious and thoughtful conversations with me. 'My appreciation to the Art Council, all members of the Board, and to the caring staff of this hospital. God bless you. God bless you.

Ebell Scholars Speech: *"Choices"*

September 11, 2014
By Dr. Elaine "Sunny" Walker

Students, as you are recognized as an Ebell Scholarship Recipient, know that in this moment, you are shaping history. You are building your personal history and you are contributing to your family's legacy. Scholars, you are, at each academic milestone, influencing the history of higher education in America. You are changing the statistics that reflect successful matriculation rates, graduation rates, and the types of degrees earned. Learning to think, learning how to apply what you learn, will shape your world. You have made *a choice* to learn. You have decided to influence, for good, professions, movements, institutions, countries, neighborhoods, and hearts. Your choices today will impact the future.

Those who are investing *in* you are counting *on* you to make good choices.

The Ebell Scholarship is a vote of confidence in your potential. You are supported because The Ebell is willing to trust you to achieve as a scholar and to, with dignity, represent this organization and your academic institution. You now have the responsibility to cause progress. Those of us who have walked where you walk now, we believe in you.

I encourage you to finish what you start. Earn your bachelor's degree. Some of you will continue on to earn graduate and doctoral degrees. Others will do specialized work that requires targeted training or experience. Some of you will discover or create unique ways to share talents and ideas with the world. Ultimately, each of you can enrich lives. Your work that qualified you for the Ebell Scholarship, suggests that you are serious about your future. And we celebrate you tonight. Let's give these students a round of applause.

About two decades ago, I was an Ebell Scholar. I am deeply grateful for the experience gained and for their financial support of my education. Unfortunately, I had to also utilize loans as I *continued* my education through the master's degree and the doctorate. Trust me, scholarships are the **better** way to go. The debt from school loans is such a burden! Students, cherish this Ebell Scholarship! It's not a hand-out. You must earn it. Good grades are *required* for continued support. Keep your grades up. Do your part. The Ebell, and your family, and others are counting on you.

Speaking of family, my parents were beautifully and fully present in my life. They contributed in every way that they could, and I honor my father and mother tonight. I was fortunate to have the truest wealth, which is love. I am blessed to have the love of family and friends. Their love is priceless. Love sustains you when you don't have money. Love inspires your heart to keep pumping when you are shocked at the cost of ever-rising college expenses, and you get those bills! Thank you, family and friends, for the love and support that both humbled me and kept me strong. Faith in God gave me the necessary confidence to keep going forward after the reality of tuition, room & board, books and other university costs tried to insist that I could not possibly partake in my dream of a good education.

When I was at USC, the Ebell stood by me. I was able to purchase books and take care of some basic campus expenses. That support was so necessary for me, and students like me. I speak now for students who have the ability to excel academically, the heart to serve, and the drive to succeed, *but* don't have the money to pay for tuition *plus* the many costs associated with university and college attendance. These students are too often forced by lean resources to quit school, to suffer disgrace, to give up on their dreams. The student suffers. The world they hope to improve suffers. We all suffer. The Ebell Scholarship Committee has worked for many decades to ease that suffering and to support promising students. Let's give the Ebell Organization a round of applause.

To show your personal gratitude to the Ebell, students, make the academic progress required, and earn that degree! If you do not already know how you want to lead or serve, begin tonight to think about it. You are now part of an amazing group, distinguished by its concern for others. The Ebell cares about you. What do *you* care about? Will your choices reflect the good? What will *you* say with *your* life?

As a scholar you will face difficult times. Do not give up. As you achieve, people (haters) will criticize. Don't invest in hate. Albert Einstein said...

> "Arrows of hate have been shot at me, but they never hit me, because somehow they belong to another world with which I have no connection whatsoever".

Disconnect from destructive communities and negative language. Fill your mind with positive thoughts. Decide right now that you will move forward with dignity and purpose. Chose to make a positive difference in this world.

As you "Indulge in the pleasant occupation of thinking", as Einstein suggested, your worldview expands and changes. You begin to think about building, finding cures, empowering others. As you become more thoughtful, you care about living responsibly, you notice the good more often. As you study and observe the world, you see the complexity and beauty in life and living things. You approach problem-solving with creativity and imagination. You demonstrate respect, and you wonder how you can make things better. *Joy finds you*. When you think, you change the structure of your brain. A well-exercised brain grows strong. Think about the choices you have, the good that you can do, then figure out a way to do it!

This special day can take on new significance for you. Will it be a new beginning? Will you invest in the world of ideas and possibilities? Will you choose to believe in yourself and in the value and potential of others? Will you commit to making the world better? Choose, this day, to redirect your thinking toward healthy, constructive endeavors. Decide right now, to be more grateful, to be part of a solution. You are here for a reason, living on a planet that is strategically suspended in space. Ponder this as you walk respectfully through this awesome world. Being here is a privilege. This world awaits your unique contribution. Choose, this day, to make a difference, your difference. May God grant you a full life, and the strength and wisdom to choose well.

Light

Speech delivered at the University of Southern California
McNair Scholars Research Conference, June 9, 2007
by Elaine Walker, Ed.D.

Albert Einstein (Physicist, 1879-1955) said, "I never think of the future. It comes soon enough". Einstein worked for many years to develop his general theory of relativity, represented by the now famous equation:

$$E = mc^2$$

Einstein suggested that the energy within an object equals its mass times the speed of light squared. He postulated that time is relative, not a constant. This theory, now proven to be accurate, began as an idea. This important work began as Einstein's dissertation proposal. I am here today to encourage you to pursue the doctorate, to write a dissertation, and to, perhaps, change the way the world thinks. I want you to think of the future.

Einstein's discovery was the result of years of study and effort. He could not have made such a discovery unless he was committed to the future. The nature of learning and discovery encompasses the "right now", for example, the activity of current research, and it considers the future – the outcome of research. Your effort today must be motivated by tomorrow. For some in the world, tomorrow is perceived as a concept that is never fully realized. For McNair Scholars, tomorrow is real. Tomorrow can mean years from this moment, when you become a doctor with an earned terminal degree.

The moment that you set an honorable academic goal, you invest in the future. The intangible goal becomes a new reality. What was once an idea can become a degree in your hand, then an instrument of light when you put that degree to work. Each scholar can transform their lives and the lives of others. It begins with a decision to try. Believing in tomorrow got you from kindergarten to college. Continue to believe, work hard, and look forward.

Those who pursue careers as Doctors of Philosophy (Ph.D.), Doctors of Education (Ed.D.), have the responsibility of providing perpetual light in their fields of exploration. Perhaps your research, your life's work, will result in findings as significant as Einstein's. Maybe you will fall in love with the pure delight of discovery. Hopefully, you will realize the purpose of your own light. Henry David Thoreau said, "To him whose elastic and vigorous thoughts keeps pace with the sun, the day is a perpetual morning". The McNair Scholars program celebrates light that is fueled by curiosity, imagination, effort, and that "perpetual morning".

I was a McNair Scholar at USC. I was the first USC McNair Scholar to earn the doctorate. I began teaching at the university in 2001. After I earned a doctoral degree, I spent a great deal of time helping students to develop or complete their dissertations. Over the years, I collaborated with researchers on a variety of projects and presentations. I was exposed to many different fields of study. This exposure helped me to realize that there is an exquisite interconnectedness linking many disciplines. Some of you in the audience are renaissance scholars. You are fascinated by, and can excel in, more than one area of study. Others will prefer to become an expert in one discipline. Either path is good. I encourage you to look for light wherever your interests lead you. Do not fear expanding your research to include others from outside of your primary discipline. Allow the intrigue and the different perspectives. Our shared goal is finding answers, making the world better. Such undertakings are not easy. Do not fear failure for it is a great teacher. Do not fear your own inner light; it is a gift from God.

Light illuminates our dark world. A career that allows you to reflect light and provide light to others is a noble use of your professional time. After you earn your doctorate, you may have the option to teach at the university level, to conduct research, and to help the world understand and benefit from your area of study. To teach is to share light. Through research, you pursue light. Robert Collyer wrote, "God hides some ideal (light) in every human soul. At some time in our life, we feel a trembling, fearful longing to do some good thing. Life finds its noblest spring of excellence in this hidden impulse to do our best." Scholars, I challenge you today to do your personal best with your life. I encourage each of you to look for and honor the light, first in yourselves, and always in others. It might take a while to discover exactly what you want to do. Ask questions. Observe. Intern. Be patient. As Louis de Buffon said: "Patience is genius".

I suggest that the focus of your academic and professional goals be not fame, but light. I quote, "Fame has this great drawback, that if we pursue it, we must direct our lives in such a way as to please the fancy of men, avoiding what they dislike and seeking what is pleasing to them". This predicament is never ending for the famous. So said Benedict Spinoza in the 17th Century. The doctorate or the doctor might be subjects of fame, but I caution you, do not make fame a primary occupation. Instead focus on the light. Do research that sheds light. How will your field advance over the next 20 years? How will your work shape the field, or change what we know? You can make a difference. You, and your light.

Each discipline is an expression of light that uses its own language and procedures to help define and serve our world. Through contributions from research, we are learning more about everything. Oh, God's magnificent earth! In it, so much to discover. Beyond it, so much to discover!!!

My greatest professional joys are found in exploring and appreciating the complexity of our world as we know it and as we dare to imagine it. A career in research opens the door to world citizenship. It carries us out of the limited corridors of small thinking, into...EVERYWHERE!! It frees us to wander outside of our known neighborhoods, into the universe. Socrates said, "I am not an Athenian nor a Greek but a citizen of the world". Yes Socrates, me too.

A career as a Researcher, Teacher, or Leader in Higher Education will empower you to share your light and to cultivate the light in others. This is awesome work. It is also humbling work. Academic Doctors are not like

George Eliot's rooster who thought the sun had risen to hear him crow. No. Our aim is to be more like the great and humble Jesus whose personal light as a teacher was so profound, that the world still speaks of it more than 2,000 years after he walked on earth.

Richard Feynman, physicist and Nobel Laureate, was also an amateur artist, a musician in a Samba band and a family man. In his book, The Pleasure of Findings Things Out (1999) he wrote, "…another value of science is the fun called intellectual enjoyment which some people get from reading and learning and thinking about it, and which others get from working in it". He also wrote, "With more knowledge comes deeper, more wonderful mystery, luring one on to penetrate deeper still. Never concerned that the answer may prove disappointing but with pleasure and confidence, we turn over each new stone to find unimagined strangeness, leading on to more wonderful questions and mysteries – certainly a grand adventure!"

Be a conscious part of the grand adventure. Decide today, or again, to jump in. The world needs you. Dive into the world of ideas and possibilities. Find a cure. Solve a problem. As someone wise once said, "Live a life of purpose where your greatest passion for good meets the world's greatest needs".

Dear scholars, I wish you glowing success as I leave you with the words of my personal hero, Jesus:

"Let your light so shine before men, that they may see your good works, and glorify your father which is in heaven" (Matthew 5:16).

-End-

Love, Language, God, and Gender

by Elaine Patricia Walker

Love, confined to human expression, never experiences all of its glory, all of its strength. Love loses some of its potency whenever it travels through the mortal effort of language. Words have limits, yes, but words are a practical choice as we attempt to discuss love. I encourage conversation about love because although people, at our best, offer only an inadequate representation of God's true love, we need to speak of it. It matters.

I have selected love as that which is most valuable to me. I have selected something that I cannot fully explain. I acknowledge that human beings may never be able to explain love precisely. We receive it, we give it, we enjoy it. We are tortured by imperfections in its delivery. We want it. We do not necessarily comprehend it. This is a mystery, isn't it?

We can say what love is not. For example, love is not murder. We can say what love produces. But we cannot point to one tangible object and rightly label it "love". Still, most people would agree that love exists. How do we come to this conclusion? We say that love is, because we seek it or we feel it. How similar this view to that of the many who have tried to explain God.

Author Elizabeth Johnson refers to philosopher Thomas Aquinas and identifies with his "working rule that we can know that God is and what God is not, but not what God is" (She Who Is, 7). In the Christian Bible, God seems knowable. God is called Creator, Father, and He is described: "God is love".

In this discussion I will follow the assumption that God and love define each other. Love, like God, is different from the things it produces or causes. Love is not health or family, not vocational success or respect. Love, at times escaping ample description, is more than its effect. Love contributes to good health, builds strong families, celebrates success and can inspire respectful behavior. But love is not anything else. Love can be compared to other things and concepts. Analogies abound. But the comparisons are not the thing compared.

Crerar Douglas, Professor of Religion at the University of Southern California in February 1996, suggested that love might be relabeled "respect", in light of "our difficult world". His theory is "that it is, in our difficult world, more important right now to say that respect is the center of human values. Love as respect". I agree that respect is crucial, right now and always. But respect is not love.

Love does not become something else to accommodate a difficult world. Love is a constant. It must be. Love is love, even when it is mistaken for something else, something that seems more attainable. Professor Douglas writes, "Everyone knows love is the center of all human values". If love is the center, and I strongly agree that it is, then nothing else is the center; not respect, not health, not you, not me. While love can be interpreted differently by a variety of people, it will always be love. Love as respect or anything else is not love.

Love is not reduced to the adjectives used to describe it. Love does not morph for our convenience. If we label love something else, we are not dealing with love. We are then dealing with the label. Word choices are important. Words are helpful as we navigate life with or without love. Words, however, are not love. Words like "I love you" need to be said if true. However, even without the sometimes-beneficial noise of spoken language, love can still be expressed, in silence or deed. A gentle, welcome embrace or a smile. A quiet act of kindness. Support and caring and connection. But for this discussion, words are key.

Elizabeth Johnson's words, in her book She Who Is, invited me to ponder the complexities of love and language. The author introduces herself to the reader as a "white middle class…and hence privileged citizen in a wealthy Northern American country" (p. 11). I am a black woman who has, like Elizabeth, travelled to continents around the world, received a university education, and noticed the inequities of the church I love. We have both worked closely with religious leaders, all males in top leadership positions within their denominations. We both have something to say about God and women.

I have loved a God, a Christ, and a Holy Spirit all referred to by my church in masculine terms. Pulpits and top leadership roles in the church are male dominated. Elizabeth Johnson writes what I know to be true: there are certainly political inequities in the Christian church, Catholic and Protestant.

While I can relate to some of Johnson's argument, I disagree with her assertion that God should be referred to as "She". Johnson appears to interpret gender referencing as a key way to rid religion of the male-oriented slant on worship and language about God. A switch to predominantly female references to God is just as limiting as the masculine references. Men have used the male categorizations longer perhaps because they snatched the power first. It may well be that women would commit the same sin if we had the opportunity, given the flaws inherent in human nature.

In Johnson's book, from the introduction on page 5 to the epilogue on page 273, she asks, "What is the right way to speak about God?" If our goal is to prove that God is as much female as male, then we can look to his creation of both man and woman, made lovingly in his image. Language, and how we speak about God and love are very important. Referring to an all-inclusive God as "She" instead of "He" excludes the He-ness of God. It is interesting that the word "She" contains the word "he", but "He" alone does not include the word "She". The word "He" does not include the feminine.

In the church to which I belong, women are not afforded the same opportunities as men. Not yet. I still love the God my church worships. The male-dominated power and political structures are unfair, but God is not.

Why does gender get in the way of speaking God's word or doing God's work?

Through my research, I discovered that leaders in my denomination believe that one of the main reasons male-preferred church leadership is upheld is because Jesus came to the earth in a male body. Jesus and God are one. Jesus is the part of God that He wanted humans to see. Jesus' mother was important. The women who followed and supported Jesus during his ministry were important. But Jesus was male in form. It is that simple. And that complicated.

God loves humans, male and female. God is pure love. When that love is mingled with people, it improves humanness, but it loses its strongest holy voice in the process. The pure love gets deposited into an impure receptacle (humans). We do our best to speak wisely about love and God. We still don't have it all figured out.

I would rather spend most of my time loving God and trying to love others in ways acceptable to God. Assigning one gender or another to God is not a priority for me. I can see the problem with constant and pervasive male references and privilege in the church and outside of the church. We continue to try to right this wrong. Firemen are now firefighters, policemen are now called police officers, and so on. Good. Women are more fairly represented when we use inclusive language and titles, which must be preceded by inclusive practices. We should not have moved from Fireman to Firewoman. Firefighter is a better choice. The challenge is applying this same inclusiveness to the identity of God.

The creator is greater than the created. With words crafted by humans, I am not confident that we will ever be able to completely articulate God's fullness of identity. Despite this inability to fully explain God, I trust that God is. I do not think that God is either female or male. I think that God exists above gender. I accept that I can know God through the world God created, and through relationship, even though I might not be able to elucidate beyond my faith. In the meantime, as I try to find the words, I can share something marvelous that I don't fully understand: I can love.

Citations

Johnson, E. A. (1995, 1992), She Who is. New York, NY: The Crossroad
    Publishing Company.

Zondervan (1985). The New International Version Bible. Grand Rapids, MI.
    Zondervan Publishing Corporation.

Max Weber's Theory of Charismatic Authority
Applied to Jesus of Nazareth

by Elaine Walker, Ed.D.

Overview

Max Weber defines *charisma* as "a certain quality of an individual personality, by virtue of which he is set apart from ordinary men and treated as endowed with supernatural, superhuman, or at least, specifically exceptional qualities…". (Eisenstaedt on Weber. xviii).

Charisma is a Greek word, present in the writings of Paul (also known as Saul of Tarsus), the famously converted Apostle of Jesus (The New Testament Scriptures, *Christian Bible*). As Paul uses the word, *charisma* connotes extraordinary giftedness. Weber considered Paul's writings in the development of his theory of Charismatic Authority.

I will apply Weber's theory of Charismatic Authority to Jesus, the famous teacher from Nazareth who remains one of the most celebrated figures in human history. I selected the historical figure Jesus because he embodies Weber's charismatic ideal.

Application Method

In this paper, I use a direct association approach. I match details of Jesus' life to Weber's criteria. I provide Weber's claim, then I explain how the experiences of Jesus, and reactions to Jesus, satisfy the claim.

Claims

The charismatic is often a marginal man with humble or disadvantaged beginnings. Scholars classify Jesus as a "Mediterranean Jewish peasant" (Crossan. *Jesus*, xii). References to Jesus as the son of a carpenter, in a society where sons often worked in the same trade as their fathers, would place Jesus on the level of artisan. These classifications of the Mediterranean working poor were common during the time that Jesus lived. Jesus was born before 4 B.C.E. Jesus grew up in Nazareth, a hamlet of about 200 people. He had at least six siblings. His people were the poorest of the Jews in the area (Johnson. *The Real Jesus*. 4).

A charismatic leader often has a troubling or questionable relationship with, or response to, his father. There is enduring debate about the identity of Jesus' father. It is a man named Joseph who weds Mary, the mother of Jesus, while she is pregnant with Jesus. By all accounts, Joseph is not the biological father of Jesus. Mary told Joseph that she became pregnant during their betrothal period, before Joseph ever had sex with her (see the Book of Luke, Chapter 1, verses 26-31 and 34-35. *Christian Bible*). Betrothal was as binding as the actual marriage, broken only by divorce. (*Spirit Filled Life Study Bible*: Page 1405, Footnotes). In the Bible's Book of Matthew, we read that Joseph did not have sex with Mary until after Jesus was born (Chapter 1, verses 18-25. *Christian Bible*).

Some historians suggest that Jesus' father could have been a Roman soldier who raped Mary. There is no proof of that claim. Remarkably, Joseph assumed a protective role, guarding Mary's dignity and her very life. Joseph honored their engagement, although he knew he had not gotten Mary pregnant. According to Jewish law, he could have exposed Mary's pregnancy, which would have led to her death by public stoning. Instead, Joseph married Mary and stayed with her until his death. Joseph assumed the role of father to the young Jesus, under controversial circumstances.

Joseph was present at the beginning of Jesus' life, quite memorably at his birth, and during Jesus' youngest years. There is no specific mention of Joseph after Jesus is age 12, when Joseph scolded Jesus for not returning with the family caravan, following a trip to Jerusalem for the Feast of the Passover. After the religious festivities, Mary and Joseph lost track of Jesus for two days. Eventually, they found him in the temple talking with the elders. Jesus responded to his parents, "Why did you worry and search for me? Didn't you know that I would be at my father's house?" Here, at age 12, Jesus was relaying that his father is God, not Joseph. How did that statement by Jesus affect the relationship between Joseph and Jesus?

Biblical scholars and historians assume that Joseph died when Jesus was a teenager as there is no mention of Joseph in the adult years of Jesus (Crossan). Jesus was Mary's eldest son. In the Jewish tradition of that time, the eldest son would learn and sustain the family's trade. He had various religious, social, and familial responsibilities (Maiscott, 13-16). The father and the eldest son were central to the family unit. Scripture and historical documents would reference Joseph if he were around during Jesus' last three explosive years. Mary, the mother, was the only parental reference in Jesus' adult years. What did Jesus experience after the death of Joseph? How did Joseph's death affect Jesus?

What happened to Jesus on a psychological level? Did his mother Mary tell Jesus that Joseph was not his biological father? If so, what age was Jesus when he learned this? Was Jesus age 12 or 30? Could this news have caused

227

a psychological upheaval that influenced the development of the charismatic?

Taken outside of the context of the Christian faith, there is mystery surrounding the identity of Jesus' biological father. Jesus focused intensely on the subject of his father, throughout the three years of his public ministry that preceded his murder. During these years especially, Jesus insisted that his father is God, not Joseph, the husband of his mother.

According to Weber, certain conditions of societal crisis must exist to set the stage for the charismatic to emerge. **"Crisis must be deep and comprehensive. Economic and political structures, and very important, moral/religious values must be in crisis. The legitimacy of the leadership must be in question. An identity crisis must occur, simultaneously, involving both the charismatic personally, and the society collectively. The oppressed or dissatisfied society looks for a savior. When a society in crisis connects with a charismatic who himself is dealing with internal crisis, the result can be a fit of large proportions. The charismatic leader is in a position to share his message and that message is likely accepted during such a time when the society seeks rescuing, revenge, or change".**

Jesus emerged during a time of intensive messianic expectation (Ward. *Jesus and His Times*, 19). Greco-Roman and Jewish history in the first quarter of Jesus' century describes the Jewish homeland as a colony of the Roman Empire. This homeland included the land bridge between Syria to the north and Egypt to the south. Jesus lived in conquered territory; a political unit ruled either by Roman governors or indirectly by Herodian rulers (Crossan. *Jesus*, 22). Most Jewish people in the region wanted their freedom from Roman rule. The stage was set.

Rome permitted freedom of religion but did not allow political action in the empire. Rome expected Jewish religious leaders to "keep the peace" among their people. When dissent occurred, the Jewish rulers usually chose to chastise their own, trying to prevent Rome's involvement in Jewish affairs. They knew that Rome was notorious for annihilating their opposition (mass killings, at worst), torture (most common), and removing privilege (a constant threat to Jewish leaders). In Palestine, where politics and religion were inseparable, it was complicated, and schisms intensified (Maiscott. *Religious Conflict and the Mission of the Messiah.* 23).

Jesus was not a politician, but the Jewish leaders deemed his actions politically threatening. Jesus did not seek political office or advancement in official religious circles. He did not seek riches or Rome's favor. In stark contrast to the Jewish leaders, Jesus befriended social outcasts, he encouraged the poor, and Jesus was particularly compassionate to compromised and abused women.

Writings indicate that Jesus became an expert on the Jewish scriptures and prophetic histories. He became a respected teacher of Jewish religious law. He had deep insights into human behavior, nature, and his people's expectations.

After Jewish authorities prevented him from speaking in the synagogues, Jesus drew massive crowds, preaching to thousands in public spaces. Jesus became the most popular of all Rabbis, with no formal education credentials and no official standing or title among the religious elite. Jesus outmatched the Jewish potentates in every regard, especially in oratory and kindness. Jesus offended the Jewish religious leaders who wanted to keep their place as authorities among their people. Jesus publicly condemned the Pharisees and Sadducees for various offenses, including moral shortcomings and complacency with unjust practices. Jesus' message of a new life was radical, disruptive. People began to follow him in droves.

Jesus lived in a setting of strict protocol and hierarchies. Jesus did not assign human value according to wealth, lineage, profession, ties to political power, or gender. He welcomed everyone! Increasingly, common Jewish people began to wonder if Jesus could be the anticipated Messiah. Some hoped he could be the leader that would help to win freedom from Roman oppression. He had an urgency about him that met their desire for change.

Jesus had an internal crisis. He grew up under Roman domination where crucifixion scenes were common. He announced in advance of his death that crucifixion was his fate. Before his arrest, his human body suffered from the toil of constant travel, and he had to manage the intense psychological pressure of false accusations, murder attempts, betrayal by friends, unwanted celebrity and fame, and frequent physical exhaustion. He had a short amount of time to change the world forever. That is internal crisis, indeed.

The leader who becomes charismatic is the one who can inadvertently or deliberately tap the reservoir of relevant myths in his culture and who knows how to draw upon these myths that are linked to its sacred figures, to its historical and legendary heroes..." (Willner. *Spellbinders*. 62). Jesus recited stories of the culture that intrigued and comforted the crowds. He related ancient and respected scripture directly to his identity and his purpose (Luke 4:16-22, *Christian Bible. Torah*). Jesus mentioned his identity as the Son of David. David is a cherished religious icon in Jewish history. Joseph, the man who raised Jesus as a child, traced his ancestry to David, as did the mother of Jesus. By making this connection, Jesus linked himself to a legendary hero of his people.

He was an expert in Jewish history and sacred laws. He demonstrated brilliant mastery of prophetic scripture and its interpretation. He knew well the oral histories of his people. Jesus showed great respect for Jewish texts and traditions.

Charismatic authority…is lodged neither in office nor in status but derives from the capacity of a particular person to arouse and maintain belief in himself as the source of legitimacy. (Weber. *The Sociology of Religion*. 70). Toward the end of his very public three-year ministry, Jesus began to proclaim, "…No one can enter the kingdom of God unless they come through me" (John:10). Jesus appalled many of the religious leaders of his day with this statement. Jesus associated with outcasts, prostitutes, tax collectors and others who offended the Jewish elite. Nevertheless, throngs of people from every social class sought him and followed him. Jesus had become their hope for new leadership.

Jesus' primary message concerned "the kingdom of God". This was an entirely new kingdom – not a physical territory to be conquered in war, not a kingdom on earth, but a spiritual place where God is king. To enter this new kingdom, people must adopt a new way of thinking. Jesus encouraged the Jewish underclass to forgive their oppressors, embrace a nonviolent lifestyle, forsake the pursuit of riches as a priority, honor Jewish traditions and laws but do not emulate the Pharisees and Sadducees (the religious/political rulers of the Jews). Jesus taught people to pray as he prayed, to do works as he did, and to seek healing instead of revenge.

This was not the message of deliverance that his people expected, but the message resonated with the restless masses that wanted change. Jesus could be their king. His throne would be crafted with words. His kingdom was not of this world.

"We must look to the responses of the followers, not to the leaders, in order to know whether a charismatic relationship has been established." (Weber. Quoted by Willner. *Spellbinders*. 18).

Consider the Jewish people of Jesus' day, scattered throughout the small towns and countryside, displayed by earlier wars. Many of these people perceived Jesus as their Messiah. During his life, Jesus also persuaded some of the regions' most respected leaders and citizens. After Jesus' death, Saul of Tarsus; an educated and devout Pharisee from a respected, wealthy family, spent years persecuting people who claimed that the crucified Jesus was indeed the Messiah. After a spiritual encounter during his travels toward Damascus to arrest and punish disciples of Jesus, Saul became a believer in Jesus as the Christ and Messiah. Saul changed his name to Paul and helped to spread the message of Jesus throughout Rome, Greece, and other parts of the world.

Thousands of years after his death by crucifixion, people still see Jesus as a king. Millions love Him, and this love has transformed their lives. The faith-based kingdom that Jesus promoted was the catalyst for a legal-rational system that emerged long after he left the earth. Indirectly, Jesus built an enduring system. He did it through his followers.

The historical Jesus is Weber's most fascinating charismatic archetype. No other charismatic has so profoundly affected the world. When Jesus initially announced his divinity, many did not accept it. Debates about his identity persist well into the 21st century. Many people believe that Jesus is who he said He is.

Some do not believe. Some cannot decide. People cannot stop talking about Jesus. The name of Jesus excites passion.

Weber proposes that society makes the charismatic. Society's response to Jesus can be summed up in the words of an anonymous writer:

> "He's a poor nobody, let's ignore him. He's a radical, let's leave him.
> He's dangerous, let's fight him. He's a criminal, let's kill him.
> He's divine, let's worship Him".

This Jesus preached for only three years in a small geographic area. In this relatively short span of time, he initiated a movement that changed the world forever. The change was activated through the power of words.

Look to his followers; the ones who were with him before and immediately after his death; and look to those followers who accept Jesus as king, today. There are millions in the fold. It is great evidence for charismatic authority that Jesus could inspire such a following, and His words could sustain followers for centuries.

Jesus embodies the mystery and phenomenal nature of charismatic authority in its purest form. Throughout human history, there are many charismatic leaders, but Jesus has the longest record of active charismatic authority. Jesus' charismatic authority perpetuates and renews itself with each new believer.

Bibliography

Anton, R. and Hegland, M. (2008). Religious Resurgence. Charismatic Leadership in Messianic and Revolutionary Movements by R. Hriar Dekmejian. New York: Syracuse Press.

Crossan, J.D. (1994). Jesus. New York: Harper Collins.

Dekmejian, R. (1976). The Middle East Journal. London: University of London Press.

Eisenstaedt, S. (1968). Max Weber on Charisma. Selected Papers. Edited. Chicago, Illinois: The University of Chicago Press, Ltd.

Johnson, T.L. (1996). The Real Jesus. New York: Harper Collins.

Maiscott, M. (1992). Religious Conflict and the Mission of the Messiah. Oxford University Press.

New International Bible and Oxford Study Bible Reference. (1985). Grand Rapids, Michigan. International Bible Society.

Ward, K. (1992). Jesus and His Times. Oxford University Press.

Weber, M. (Date unavailable). Collected Essays in the Sociology of Religion. In Religionssoziologie. Translated by E. Fischoff. Boston, Mass. Beacon Press, Publisher.

Weber, M. (1968). Max Weber on Charisma and Institution Building. Charisma and Institutionalization in the Sphere of Religion and Culture. The Sociology of Charismatic Authority. Chicago, IL. The University of Chicago Press.

Weber, M. (1978). Max Weber: Selections in Translation. Translated by E. Matthews. Great Britain: University Press, Cambridge.

Understanding Paul's Chains

by Elaine Patricia Walker, Ed.D.

Paul, formerly Saul of Tarsus, is one of the most notable apostles of Jesus. A respected religious figure in Jewish circles of his time, Paul provided a wealth of written material for scholars to consider. His letters, teachings, and sermons document the organization of the early Jesus-centered church established among Gentile populations in and around Rome, years following the crucifixion of Jesus.

Christian religions find great value in Paul's known writings, and historians find his material useful as a commentary on society, power, economics, and the politics of Paul's day. Paul's writings provide guidance for church organization and rationale for Christian moral reasoning in the context of community. Paul's writings also include the topic of slavery.

Paul described himself as a man chained to the gospel; a slave for the cause of Christ. Paul was also familiar with a different kind of slavery – a slavery that involved far more than metaphor. In this paper, I will discuss Paul's experience with the run-away slave named Onesimus. The account is recorded in the book of Philemon in the Christian bible. (Reference: Verses 8-17, *The Epistle of Paul to Philemon*. New Testament. NIV, p.1486). Paul's friend Philemon was a slave owner.

Paul's teachings on the subjects of freedom, brotherhood, and human rights referred to the ideal of liberty through Jesus, the Christ. Paul spoke of a figurative freedom for all men. In Paul's day, personal freedom, political, economic and social freedom was reserved for full Roman citizens and free men of the regions under Roman rule, not for slaves.

To understand Paul's view on slavery, we must first understand that slavery in Paul's day was different from slavery practiced in modern North America (in The United States of America).

Professor S. Scott Bartchy writes of slavery in Paul's day, "Racial factors played no role, education was greatly encouraged for males, slaves could own property – including other slaves, and the majority of urban domestic slaves could legitimately anticipate being emancipated by the age of 30" (The Anchor Bible, v.6, p.66, *Greco-Roman Slavery in the New Testament*).

Essayist Lloyd A. Lewis, an African American, suggests that we should dissect Paul's language to gain insight regarding Paul's view on slavery and how he handled relations with slaves and slave owners. Lewis studies the linguistic relationship between Paul, Philemon, and Onesimus. He describes the relationship as "fraught with the social barriers that stand between a master and his slave" (in *An African-American Appraisal of the Philemon-Paul-Onesimus Triangle*). Lewis' interpretation of Paul's letter to Philemon is influenced by his intense study of the language of slavery. Lewis argues that a master would speak differently than a slave and far more freely. One man owns his tongue, the other does not.

Lewis suggests that Paul's letter to Philemon regarding Onesimus is a clear illustration of the inequities of that society. Paul, as a free man, spoke to Philemon on behalf of Onesimus.

Onesimus had no recognized, legal voice at that time. Onesimus was Philemon's slave. Onesimus was a run-away slave who went to Paul for help. Paul wrote a letter to Onesimus' "master", but Paul did not denounce slavery. Paul asked Philemon to have mercy on Onesimus. Paul encouraged Onesimus to return to his master's household. By law then, Philemon could have killed Onesimus for running away. Even though Paul spoke of himself as a "slave" for the gospel, Paul was clearly not a slave in the same way that Onesimus was a slave.

Paul's goal was to win people to faith in Jesus: Jesus as the resurrected savior of the world. Becoming a follower of Jesus did not change social status. Paul saw no reason why it should. Paul believed that the world of his day would come to an end in his lifetime. With that eschatological view, Paul thought that all worldly realities would soon perish. Challenging slavery, only one injustice among many in Paul's day, would seem to Paul a misuse of his limited time. Paul preached his gospel with urgency. He taught churches and won people to the faith. This was his focus. Paul's evangelistic mission and religious fervor outweighed whether a person was rich or poor, free or slave.

Paul's letter to Philemon was not an attempt to address the evils of slavery. The letter was an appeal made on behalf of a fellow convert. Paul probably believed that Philemon would not kill Onesimus. The most optimistic view is that Paul hoped his slave-owning friend would forgive Onesimus and receive him afresh as a brother in the faith. Paul confirmed that Onesimus accepted Jesus as the Christ, and that they now all shared the same faith. Paul then sent Onesimus back to his "master".

Is Paul to be condemned because he returned Onesimus? Paul obeyed the law of the land. As a Roman citizen Paul benefitted from the law. Only a master could legally set a slave free. Slavery was legal in Paul's day and a "normal" part of life in his community. Paul believed that he was doing a noble thing in winning Onesimus to Christianity, then sending the slave back to Philemon, a fellow Christian. Evangelist, slave owner, and slave, all Christians but not all equal.

Paul wore chains. There were the physical chains Paul was forced to wear during his various arrests and imprisonment for preaching about Jesus. Perhaps the physical chains resembled the kind of chains that Onesimus wore as a returned slave, so Paul felt he could relate to Onesimus on a special level. When Paul was not in physical chains, he also wore invisible chains that kept him, as he described, shackled to the gospel. Were Paul and Onesimus really alike?

Understanding Paul's chains is important as we try to understand his ministry and his values. Why did Paul tolerate the evil of slavery – of one person "owning" another person? Paul knew that false imprisonment and unfair servitude were both wrong. Paul taught about moral behavior, didn't he? Paul focused more on the eternal promise, versus a person's lot in a temporary life on earth. Thus, Paul sought to redefine slavery, but never to abolish it.

Made in the USA
Monee, IL
23 February 2022

49127a4a-d82a-4430-9393-890a1dd4d894R01